GREEN GIFTS

GREEN GIFTS

How to turn flowers and plants into original and lasting gifts

Gill Dickinson
photography by Debbie Patterson

FULCRUM

Author's Dedication
In memory of my father, Victor Hey;
his love and knowledge of nature have been a constant inspiration.

Published by Fulcrum Books in the United States of America

Conceived, edited and designed by
Tucker Slingsby Limited
Berkeley House, 73 Upper Richmond Road,
London SW15 2SZ

Library of Congress Cataloging-in-Publication Data

Dickinson, Gill.
Green gifts : how to turn flowers and plants into original and lasting gifts / Gill Dickinson
p. cm.
Includes index.
ISBN 1-55591-397-0 (hardcover)
1. Container gardening. 2. Plants, Potted. 3. Handicraft. 4. Gifts. I. Title.
SB418.D535 1998
745.92'6--dc21 97-23567
CIP

ISBN 1-55591-397-0
Printed in Italy by Industrie per le Arti Grafiche Garzanti Verga s.r.l.
Color reproduction by Bright Arts Graphics, Singapore

Text and editorial: Stella Martin, Stephanie Donaldson, Janet Slingsby and Nicole Foster
Horticultural Consultant: Stella Martin BSc. Hort
Art Director: Prue Bucknall
Illustrations: Kate Simunek
Photography: Debbie Patterson
Additional photography: Andrew Sydenham, Liz Eddison

0 9 8 7 6 5 4 3 2 1
Fulcrum Publishing
350 Indiana Street, Suite 350
Golden, Colorado 80401-5093
(800) 992-2908 • (303) 277-1623
e-mail: fulcrum@fulcrum-gardening.com
website: www.fulcrum-gardening.com

Contents

Introduction

Festivals, celebrations, saying "happy birthday", "thank you", "congratulations" or "get well soon": there are many occasions throughout the year when you want to give someone a present. A green gift of flowers or plants, however simple or inexpensive, can be a pleasure to create and will be appreciated by your family and friends for its originality and lasting beauty. There are projects here to suit every kind of home and garden, and to suit recipients of every age and interest – including fun gifts for children to make and to receive.

Each season brings new ideas and possibilities for green gifts. If you have a garden, you will have your own supply of seeds, seedlings, flowers and foliage to use. If not, making a careful selection at the garden center or florist means you can still create lovely gifts at no great cost. And look out for natural materials when you are out walking. Moss, twigs, bark, wild grasses, seedheads, berries, and fallen leaves can all be employed to make attractive green gifts and decorations.

The right finishing touches, which complement your gift, can make the simplest present look very special. Choose interesting papers, such as a combination of brown parcel paper and colored tissue, for wrapping flowers and pots. Try using string as an alternative to ribbon, recycled cans instead of purchased containers, and baggage tags instead of expensive tags and cards.

Remember to accompany your gift with the appropriate care notes copied from the back of the book, where there is also a calendar that gives guidance on the best sowing, planting, and picking times.

SPRING

Spring generously provides a wealth of occasions to give green gifts, plus a wealth of material to create them.

Spring ideas

After a long, cold winter the greening of the garden is a small miracle – plants thrust new growth through the soil, and soon the bare earth is covered with a haze of green as the whole garden springs to life. Every day there is excitement as more plants defy the chilly nights, unfurl their leaves, and show signs of flowering. Bulbs brighten the garden, vying with one another to make the most colorful display. On warm days the air is filled with scent, and you can rediscover the pleasure of lingering outdoors.

Like the season itself, spring gifts have a freshness that is very welcome after the gloom of winter months. Clean colors, fresh scents, and crisply delicious tastes refresh and renew us all. Gifts need not be elaborate or expensive – picking sticky buds from a horse chestnut tree or a few twigs from an apple branch requires little effort if you have a tree growing in your backyard, but to someone who lives in the center of a city they are a rare and precious treat. And, left in a vase of water, many tree buds will continue to open and grow to give some weeks of interest and beauty.

This is the time when seeds are sown so put some into pretty homemade envelopes and send them to distant friends and family. They will think of you all summer as the seeds grow and flower. For neighbors and friends who live close by, suggest a competition to see who grows the best, the biggest, or the tastiest! Children will enjoy a contest to grow the tallest

Left top to bottom: Plants bought from a florist or garden center can easily be packaged to make great gifts – or you can work the same magic on plants from your own yard. Wrap small pots in colorful paper and add a bow and tag. Plant a rustic basket with violets, or give daffodil bulbs planted in a terracotta pot.

sunflower. If you sow seeds yourself, you will probably have a glut of seedlings. Make this another opportunity to give green, growing gifts to family and friends.

As you work in the yard clearing, dividing, sowing, and transplanting, plant extra pots and containers to give away either now or later in the year. In particular this is the time to replant your herb garden with annuals such as basil and chervil, and to replace any perennials that have died. Buy extra plants and pot them to give to friends who are enthusiastic cooks or indeed to anyone who will enjoy the scents of herbs like mint or rosemary in their kitchen or garden.

In spring it isn't only gardens that are bursting with new growth – garden centers and florists are crammed with pots of bulbs and vigorous young plants. Repotted or imaginatively gift-wrapped, they make perfect seasonal presents.

The holidays of spring can all be celebrated with green gifts. Red roses are traditional for Valentine's Day – instead of paying high prices at a florist, buy a potted red rose bush and hang it with red paper hearts. It may not have flowers on Valentine's Day, but it will have many in the future to remind your beloved of enduring affection. A rustic basket holding primulas or violas is a delightful Mother's Day gift that children can plant themselves with a little help. Easter eggs can look magical nestling on a bed of moss among miniature narcissus or primroses. Paint or stencil pots with appropriate motifs or messages – you will find lots of inspiring ideas in the Finishing Touches section at the end of the book.

Right top to bottom: To make Easter more special, give green gifts that will last all summer as well as the traditional, instantly eaten, eggs. Friends far away can be sent packs of seeds. Birthdays and other special occasions can be celebrated in style with the strong and vibrant colors of tulips complemented by striking gift tags.

Primroses and primulas

A rainbow display of primroses and primulas is a welcome foretaste of spring, and such colorful collections can usually be seen early in the year in most florists and garden centers. These flowers have been bred for size as well as color, but smaller and less striking ones are available if you prefer them. Individual plants in pots are not expensive so you can afford to create a great spring gift, suitable for indoors or out, by putting several plants together in a windowbox, basket, or large flowerpot.

Above: A bright primula in flower makes a welcome splash of color on an office desk or kitchen table. If the container you have chosen isn't waterproof, line it with plastic (see page 22).

Garden centers also sell boxes of six or so young plants together, either mixed or of one color, and these, too, will make excellent gifts. For those who have the space, mail-order seedlings, or "plugs," are available in larger quantities. This saves the trouble of germinating seed yourself but does require some expertise in growing the seedlings on into healthy plants.

Polyanthus, primula, or primrose – they all belong to the same family, but the naming can be confusing. Polyanthus have several flowers on the same stem and are usually taller than primroses, but they are equally good for growing in containers.

Like most spring flowers, primroses need cool, moist conditions, so keeping them in a warm room will shorten their flowering time, and they may become rather spindly in growth after a while. Outdoor containers will do best in a sheltered place, protected from extremes of wet and cold. To pass on care advice to the recipient of your gift, copy the notes on page 124.

Above: Traditional small-flowered pale yellow primroses make everyone think of spring. They can be planted in windowboxes or patio pots if the gift is going to someone with a garden. If plants are to be kept indoors, a woven rustic basket makes an attractive container. For instructions on lining baskets, see page 22. For instructions and templates for making flower tags, see pages 116 and 120.

When buying, choose plants that have healthy leaves (remove any that are yellowing or diseased) and plenty of buds. Water the pots if they are at all dry and let them stand for an hour or two before replanting.

The container should be deep and wide enough to hold the roots comfortably of as many plants as you have decided on and in a color to match or contrast with the flowers. Put plenty of drainage material, such as broken pottery or gravel, in the base of the pot, especially if there are no holes in the bottom to drain excess water. Use a peat-based potting mix and make sure the plants are firmed well in. Water them to settle the soil. Moss on the top is an attractive finishing touch if there are gaps between the plants. If possible, leave the container for a few days before giving it away, to avoid too many "shocks" at once.

Daffodils

Daffodils are the quintessential spring flowers: when the earth is still too cold for most other flowers to appear, their spears pierce the frosty soil and their golden trumpets brighten even the gloomiest day. They are one of the easiest bulbs to grow, and provided the foliage is left to die back naturally after flowering, they will multiply quickly and provide plenty of flowers for picking. Daffodils are also among the cheapest cut flowers to buy, and they are good value as they last well in water.

It is not always possible or appropriate to give a lavish gift, but an inexpensive present, given an individual touch, can be just as welcome – and daffodils are perfect for this treatment. As they are cheap to buy, it is possible to be generous and use them liberally.

When giving daffodils, whether bought or cut from your yard, it is best to select a mixture of blooms at different stages. If possible, choose some in tight bud, some beginning to open, and others fully open. This will ensure that your gift looks good for as long as possible. As with all flowers, daffodils benefit from conditioning (standing in deep water in a cool place) before they are arranged. Daffodils are unusual in that their sap has an adverse effect on other flowers, so be sure to condition them separately. To condition florist's daffodils, cut off approximately 1 inch from their stems and plunge them into cool, deep water. Home-picked flowers need no extra trimming provided they are put in water immediately after picking. Leave the daffodils to stand in a cool place for at least three hours before arranging.

A bunch of cut daffodils is a lovely, if short-lived, gift, but a pot

Above: An interesting vase is a welcome gift – especially when you demonstrate how to make a few flowers fill a large receptacle! Lichened twigs hold the flowers in place. This idea can be used with any large vase, demonstrating that you don't have to spend a fortune on flowers to fill a fashionably large vase. If you want to make the twigs more secure, tie them together with raffia.

Right: The architectural beauty of these daffodils, tied together with sisal string, transforms everyday flowers into something special. To keep the flower heads in place, hold them together with rubber bands immediately under the flowers and at the base of the stems. Bind the stems with the sisal string just above halfway up the stems. Leave the rubber bands in place until just before you present the flowers, then cut them off. This style of arrangement makes your flowers easy to transport.

Far right: Spring buds provide the perfect complement to spring flowers and often last much longer – giving a city friend the pleasure of seeing buds unfurl. A tag embellished with twigs is the finishing touch (see page 117).

of daffodils can give pleasure for many years to come. You can plant pots of bulbs in the fall ready to give as gifts in the early months of the following year (see pages 86 and 104). One advantage of doing this is that you can choose some of the more unusual varieties of daffodils that are available at garden centers and which can be hard to obtain ready-grown. Another advantage of planting extra pots of bulbs in the autumn is that you will have home-grown gifts, suitable for almost every occasion, on hand.

Not everyone has the time, space or inclination to grow their own bulbs, but garden centers and florists are well aware of this and you will have no difficulty in buying inexpensive pots of daffodils and narcissus in bud. Choose plants where the buds are just showing. They will still look very attractive, and it means your gift will have a much longer life. Personalize purchased pots with an unusual gift wrapping (see page 112 for ideas and instructions) or replant the bulbs in decorated pots. Take care not to disturb the roots, and water them after repotting. The bulbs should flower indoors or out, unless you are in a very cold region. When choosing and decorating a pot, bear in mind whether the bulbs are likely to end up indoors or outside. Daffodils for outdoors need to be in sturdy pots. For ideas on painting and decorating pots, see page 118.

You can remind the recipient that your gift of daffodil bulbs has an added bonus: they should flower again next year. So put in a reminder either to stand the pot in a shady corner and leave the foliage to die back or to plant the bulbs outside. You can also give the care notes on page 127 for bulbs in flower with your gift.

Left: A bunch of daffodils or narcissus can be turned into a memorable gift by a little attention to the wrappings. Here, a simple bunch of narcissus has been wrapped in brown paper lined with yellow tissue and tied with raffia. An evergreen leaf completes the design. Daffodils, enhanced by the addition of stems of twisted willow, are wrapped in brown paper loosely tied with green tissue and bound with some more twisted willow. For instructions see page 112.

Top right: Don't despair if you didn't plant pots in the fall – many bulbs are available to buy in pots and can easily be transplanted into decorative containers.

Center right: A purchased pot of daffodils or narcissus can be enhanced by a spectacular wrapping. See page 112 for instructions.

Bottom right: Put purchased bulbs into unusual containers for an off-beat gift. Twig supports pushed into the pot add interest.

Seed packs & seedlings

Spring finds gardeners hard at work planting seeds and looking after seedlings. Packs of seeds make a great gift for gardening friends who live far away, since the seeds can easily be sent through the mail. They are also inexpensive, so they make perfect presents for children to send to grandparents or give on Mother's or Father's Day. Your surplus seedlings are less easy to transport, but will make a welcome present for neighbors and friends who live close by. With a little thought these gifts can be chosen to reflect the interests and expertise of the recipient. So, for example, cooks are given culinary herbs and children easy-to-grow annuals.

When giving purchased seeds, leave them in their own pack, which will have all the detailed instructions on it for growing. But this pack can be put inside an envelope you have decorated yourself. If delivery is not a problem, add a seed tray and a small bag of potting soil. The seeds do not have to be bought, of course – you can collect them from your own plants (or from

Right: Make your own colorful seed packs. Choose brightly colored envelopes and add your own decorations – these can range from photographs of your garden in full bloom to pictures cut from magazines. Or, if children are sending the gift, get them to paint their own picture of flowers or vegetables on the pack. Instructions for the wire and tissue motifs on these packs are given on page 116. If you are giving home-grown seeds you may want to include the care notes given on page 124.

Left: This collection of seedlings makes a great gift for someone who wants to try growing his or her own salads or vegetables. For a friend with a patio full of containers to plant, give lobelia, petunia, alyssum, impatiens and nasturtium seedlings. For someone who likes to cut flowers for the house, give seedlings such as bachelor's buttons, larkspur, helichrysum, and cosmos. If you want to give care notes with your gift of seedlings, see page 124.

friends' plants, provided you have their permission). However, there are advantages to commercially grown seed: it is of high quality and will grow true. It is also clean and ready to plant.

Special collections of seeds are available, but it is more interesting to make up your own selections:

Child: hardy annuals such as nasturtium, sunflower, candytuft, Virginia stock; easy vegetables such as radish.

Vegetable grower: unusual varieties of tomato, lettuce, beans, or brassica.

Enthusiastic gardener: less common forms of perennials; also shrubs and trees from specialized catalogs.

Nature-lover: wildflower seeds, either mixed or singly.

You can also give seeds to reflect a color theme – all white or all blue, for example.

A surplus of seedlings provides gardeners with the chance to give a welcome gift. You can also buy pots of seedlings, such as sweet peas, in garden centers and divide them up yourself or get trays of "plugs" by mail order. Before giving seedlings, make sure you have nursed them to a state where they are likely to survive. It is best to give seedlings once they have been pricked out (transplanted) into small individual pots. Very tiny ones, such as lobelia, can be put in little clumps quite happily. Keep them well watered and in a sheltered place for a week or two to allow them to settle down and become established before giving them away.

To make your seedlings more of a special gift, look out for interesting and appropriate containers in which to deliver the little pots.

Easter

Spring flowers and plants make ideal companions – or substitutes – for traditional Easter gifts such as candy eggs and fluffy toy chicks. There is a huge range of spring flowers to choose from at this time of year, including bulbs (daffodils and narcissus are especially good), azaleas, lily-of-the-valley (wonderfully scented), primroses, and bedding plants such as pansies, daisies, and forget-me-nots. In addition to the designs shown here, there are many other ideas in the book which can be adapted to create Easter presents using these plants and flowers. In particular, check out the primrose basket on page 12, the daffodil gifts on pages 14 to 17, the topiary on page 58, and the seed packs on page 18, which are perfect for popping inside an Easter card.

To underline the Easter theme, look out for appropriate garden and florist's accessories such as wire frames featuring chickens and rabbits, and for little baskets and pots which can be decorated and planted with Easter flowers. If you are planning a gathering of friends and family over Easter, make a display of plants, flowers, and other gifts as a table center. You can then hand out individual presents (chocolate eggs for the children!) to each person at the appropriate time. The purely decorative items can stay in place for everyone to enjoy over the holiday period.

Top left: This little pot of anemones is a perfect Easter present. For information on painting pots, see page 118. For details of how to make the wire and tissue bunny, leaves, and flower, see page 116.
Center left: A metal pot planted with trailing green ivy makes an ideal nest for Easter eggs and for a topiary hen (see opposite).
Bottom left: Easter baskets can be planted with a variety of spring flowers. Violets are shown here. See page 22 for how to line a basket.

Right: The focal points of this Easter display are a topiary hen and a wire rabbit filled with moss and planted with flowers. Easter eggs and spring blossom complete the picture. For information on using topiary frames, see page 58. To plant the rabbit, first pack the frame with moss, then line with plastic and half-fill it with soil. Choose a selection of spring plants and bulbs to plant inside. Position them and firm in with more soil. Water well and keep in a cool place.

LINING AND PLANTING A BASKET

1 Line the basket with thick black plastic, leaving an overhang of about 2 inches at the top. Using a sharp knife, make several slits for drainage in the base of the plastic, taking care not to damage the basket.

2 Water the plants about an hour before replanting them. Partly fill the basket with soilless potting medium and make a hollow for each plant. Remove the plants from their pots and place them, with the rootballs just touching, into the soil.

3 Fill in and firm around the plants with soil, just covering the tops of the rootballs. Leave a gap of about 1 inch between the soil and the top of the basket. Tuck in the edges of the plastic.

Right: A basket of violas or pansies is an ideal gift for Mother's Day or for a spring birthday as well as for Easter. And the plants inside should flourish outdoors once the first flowering is over – freeing up the basket to be planted with summer flowers! The care notes on page 124 for the primrose and primula basket can also be used for this basket.

Below: A beautifully made tag can become a keepsake in its own right. This one features pressed flower heads (see page 117 for tag instructions). The tag can also carry useful information for the gift's recipient, telling them how to care for their gift.

EASTER BASKET

A wide, fairly shallow wicker basket makes an excellent container for the cheery "faces" of violas or pansies. These will give a display for several weeks, especially if the dead flowers are regularly removed. Snip them off with scissors. Use enough plants to fill the basket without squashing the roots together.

The basket can be kept indoors in a light but cool situation, or if you give it to someone with a yard it can stand outside on a table or the top of a low wall. Indoors, it will need a dish underneath to catch any moisture, since it is important that the container is free-draining. If, on the other hand, it is to stay outside for any length of time, the basket must be painted all over with an exterior flat-finish wood preservative and left to dry before planting.

When the plants stop producing new flowers and look straggly, they can be cut back and put outdoors. Tell the recipient to plant them with a handful of fertilizer in a partly shaded place. Kept well watered, they should regrow and flower again for most of the summer.

Tulips

Give tulips for an exuberant splash of bright spring color that is guaranteed to raise a smile. Depending on the type chosen, tulips can be in flower from early March to late May, either indoors or out, and come in an enticing variety of shapes and heights. The early sorts tend to be shorter, some having beautifully marked leaves, as well as blooms which open wide in the sun and are sometimes scented.

Taller tulips in containers have a wonderful way of bending their stems in different directions, giving the arrangement a sense of movement. They may need supporting with small stakes and ties if they lean over too far; some varieties will grow leggy if they are not kept cool enough. The double-flowered ones have heavy heads and may also need supporting. For variation in shape, the lily-flowered types are especially elegant with their slim buds and pointed petals. Then there are the parrot tulips – their fringed edges giving them an exotic, feathery look.

Tulip colors range from pure white to almost black, plus there are varieties with stripes and bicolors. Choose colors and containers to complement each other. With an outdoor pot you can also put in some soft pastel spring bedding plants, such as pink and white perennial daisies, to enhance the scheme.

TOP TULIP CHOICES FOR INDOORS AND OUT

EARLY FLOWERING

Red Riding Hood
scarlet with purple marked leaves

DOUBLE FLOWERED

Monte Carlo
yellow

LILY FLOWERED

Ballerina
tangerine

PARROT

Black Parrot
chocolate

LATE FLOWERING

Aristocrat
purple edged in white

Left: Strikingly colored flowers deserve equally attractive containers. For ideas and instructions for painting and stenciling flowerpots, see page 118. For care notes to give with pots of tulip bulbs, see page 124.

Below: Plant tulip bulbs in the fall (see the care notes for planting bulbs on page 127) or, in the spring, buy pots that are ready to flower. Choose bright-colored pots and tissue paper to complement the colors. For ideas on making matching tags and greetings cards, see page 114.

Left: Many perennial herbs, such as lavender, mint, rosemary, thyme, bay, and sage, will happily live in pots in the yard and provide you with kitchen herbs faithfully year after year. This means you can keep some extra pots to give away to friends who admire your sweet-smelling and decorative herb collection. Give tender plants winter protection in a sheltered spot and keep them well watered in the summer.

Right: Plant small containers with herbs as soon as new plants are available in garden centers. These can be left to settle in and then given to friends for spring and summer birthdays and other special occasions. For care notes to accompany your gift, see page 124.

Herbs

There is nothing to beat fresh herbs for taste and scent. It is not just enthusiastic cooks who will appreciate a basket of small plants ready to nurture. Anyone with an interest in food will want to experiment with the different flavors of herb leaves snipped over salads and other dishes. Others will enjoy the scents of lavender or lemon balm in their yard or savor a cup of freshly made camomile tea. Perennial and shrubby herbs can be a lasting pleasure for years to come and, if planted in containers which are not too heavy, can even be moved to another house if necessary.

It is easy to grow many annual herbs from seed, so a few packs of seeds such as parsley, dill, basil, and cilantro, with perhaps some pots and a small bag of potting soil, would be an excellent gift (see page 18 for ideas on turning seeds into a special gift). Alternatively, you could start the seedlings off yourself and pot them, or buy young plants for the recipient to grow on and plant out. Purchased plants are probably best for the perennials such as sage, rosemary and thyme, unless you are really good at taking cuttings. One herb not to give as a present is rue, since it can cause skin burns if not handled carefully. Don't forget that herbs can include plants such as scented-leaf geraniums (pelargoniums), which come in a wide variety of delicious smells from roses to nutmeg and can also be used as a flavoring in recipes. Another unusual idea is to give a selection of one type of herb, such as basil, which can be found in a variety of flavors, some with colored and attractive leaves.

CARE OF HERBS

One of the most important considerations for growing herbs successfully is their position, which must be sheltered from cold winds and not too heavily shaded. Well-drained fertile soil is ideal, so it may be a good idea to add extra grit if your soil is heavy and also to put in plenty of well-rotted humus or a general fertilizer at the base of the hole when planting. Of course, if the herbs are grown in containers, you can

Above: A simple but special way to present a gift of herbs is to buy a small collection of plants to suit the recipient's interests and then put them together in an attractive garden basket or tray. The herb pots shown here have first been put inside brown bags decorated with gardening motifs. For a selection of gardening motifs to copy, see page 120. Some indoor herbs can be used throughout the winter, including chives, cilantro, marjoram, chervil, parsley, and mint – but warn friends to keep mint separate from the other herbs or it will swamp them.

Right: Bay and rosemary in a little basket make a lasting and useful gift for Easter, Mother's Day, or a spring birthday.

make the potting mixture to suit these requirements and then stand the pots in the best position outside. Several containers of different sizes grouped together make a very attractive feature in even a small yard, and they can be moved under cover in cold weather if necessary. You can solve present-giving problems for years to come by giving a new herb pot every spring!

HERBS FOR COOKS

Parsley
Dill
Thyme
Marjoram
Mint
Basil
French Tarragon
Cilantro
Winter and Summer Savory

FRAGRANT HERBS

Curry Plant
Creeping Thymes
Southernwood
Lavender
Lemon Verbena

HERBS FOR CONTAINERS

Mint
Tarragon
Chives
Parsley
Marjoram
Basil
Dill
Fennel
Sage
Bay
Savory

PLANTING A STRAWBERRY POT WITH HERBS

This is a very good way of having a variety of herbs when space is limited. The pot will need some replanting every year as it will become overcrowded. Include different kinds of thymes and marjorams, parsley, basil, sage, hyssop, and rosemary.

1 Put drainage material into the pot to 4-inch depth and insert a pipe pierced with holes into the center. Start to fill around it with potting soil up to the first level of holes. Push a plant (one to each hole) into the pot, tucking the roots well inside and spreading them out carefully.

2 Repeat this process to the next level of holes and then continue filling with soil to within 2 inches of the top. Use creeping herbs in the side holes and taller, upright ones in the top. Leave the end of the pipe just above the level of the soil for easy watering and feeding.

Herbs can also be grown successfully in the house, for instance in a box, ideally at least 12 inches deep, on the kitchen windowsill. Tips of shoots will need to be pinched off to prevent plants from becoming too straggly, and watch out for aphids on the leaves. Give your gift with a copy of the care notes on page 124.

All herbs grown in containers, whether indoors or out, will need watering, although overwatering can cause just as much trouble as too little. This is why well-drained potting mixture is important, as is a layer of drainage material in the bottom of the pot. As most herbs are used for their leaves, feeding is vital for strong, continuing growth. Slow-release granular fertilizers, which are mixed into the soil when planting, can be used as a substitute for regular liquid feeding.

Sunflowers

Giant sunflowers are fun for children to grow because they shoot up fast and can reach amazing heights – often more than 10 feet. They make a great present for a group of youngsters who can then compete to produce the tallest plant. For this, each child will need a pack of seeds, a small starter pot, and a bigger outdoor pot, a label, and a bag of soil. The seeds must be a variety such as "Russian Giant" or "Giant Single" to ensure good results. The large pot should be at least 12 inches across and terracotta or ceramic as the plant will be top-heavy when fully grown. For an extra-special gift, paint on the child's name or an appropriate motif (see page 118 for information on painting pots). The competition "rules" are given on page 125 so you can copy them for the participants.

Sunflowers also make good presents for adults, either as packs of seeds or as potted young plants which you have grown yourself. But give the more compact varieties in this case, which only go up to 3 feet or so and are more useful in beds. They make colorful annuals in shades of dark red, yellow, and orange, often flowering well into early autumn. A fun variety to try is "Teddy Bear," reaching only about 2 feet, but having double flowers up to 6 inches across. Varieties suitable for growing in windowboxes are now also available and can be picked to use indoors.

The seeds can be sown direct into the soil outdoors or started in gentle warmth inside for earlier blooming. Sunflowers are not fussy about conditions, provided they are in full sun.

Left and opposite: Sunflowers always look spectacular, and you can now buy seeds to grow them in many different sizes and shades. Look out for dwarf sunflowers suitable for patio pots and windowboxes – and to pick for stunning indoor arrangements. Sunflower seeds make a great gift for children: choose tall-growing varieties. You can make seed packets which double as greetings cards to hold the seeds. For a sunflower motif to copy see page 120. The seeds can either be grown in a big pot or in a sunny spot in the garden.

GOOD VARIETIES

Velvet Queen	**- deep red**
Sunburst	**- pale yellow to maroon**
Moonwalker	**- yellow with dark center**

Above: There is something about spectacular sunflowers that makes everyone smile. Give them as seeds, seedlings, or in big bunches to bring the sun into someone's day!

SUMMER

It's summer time and the giving is easy – there are so many colorful flowers and plants to pick and plant.

Summer ideas

Each gift from the summer garden is an opportunity to share some of the season's bounty with family and friends. A relative who has no yard of their own will be delighted with a posy freshly picked from the flowerbed or with a basket of fruit or tender young vegetables. A busy friend will appreciate a decorated pot overflowing with colorful summer annuals or a container of fragrant lilies just coming into flower. For a more lasting gift, try your hand at simple topiary – small-leaved ivies twined around a frame grow far more quickly than the more usual clipped topiary. Choose a frame to suit the recipient and plan your gift well in advance. The end result will make a real talking-point perched on a table in the backyard. For an unusual fun gift, perhaps for a child, plant salad vegetables and herbs in a large container. The lucky recipient can pick and eat the produce all summer long.

Summer celebrations often take place outdoors, and it adds to everybody's enjoyment if you take along a gift which makes a decorative – or edible – contribution to the occasion. To dress the table, make a sweet-smelling garland of fresh herbs or a decorative basket packed with eye-catching annuals. A container of growing alpine strawberries complete with ripe fruit to pick and eat is sure to be extremely popular. As twilight falls, flickering candles add to the pleasure of a summer's

Left top to bottom: Summer provides a wealth of flowers to give – from striking chili peppers to stylish lilies and simple mixed posies. If you are lucky you can give flowers from your own backyard, but otherwise florist's flowers can easily be given a personal touch with handmade wrappings and bows.

evening – candles in flowerpots surrounded by scented flowers make a great decoration for an outdoor party.

If you have a summer garden full of flower-packed containers and beds you will be able to rustle up a green gift in a flash. You can give one of your own planted pots or pick a little bunch of herbs or flowers. Even if you have no yard of your own, you can still give your friends green gifts by buying a houseplant or a bunch of summer flowers and adding your own individual finishing touches. Put the plants in pots you have painted or decorated yourself. Cover the soil around the plant with smooth stones or moss, use twisted willow or hazel as plant supports instead of the usual bamboo stakes and for a final flourish, tie a large raffia or ribbon bow around the pot. Instead of paying the florist to put together an arrangement, buy bunches of seasonal flowers and foliage and do it yourself. Wrap the flowers in layers of tissue paper chosen to complement their color, tie with ribbon, and add a handmade gift tag. None of these touches is complicated or expensive, but they make all the difference.

Summer proceeds at a different pace in different places and in different years. Rain and cold can make flowers appear much later some years than others. Keep an eye on your yard if you want to pick flowers or herbs for drying or want to save seeds to grow or give away. To make lavender bottles (see page 66) you need to pick the lavender stalks while they are still green and flexible. To gather lavender and other flower heads for drying, choose a dry, sunny day. Herbs for drying or freezing are best picked just before the plant comes into full bloom: choose leaves in good condition.

Right top to bottom: There is a green gift to suit every summer occasion – from attractive containers to adorn someone's patio, to houseplants for friends with no backyard at all. For outdoor summer parties, candles surrounded by flowers and foliage make a delightful gift.

Climbing frames

Supports or frames fitted inside containers mean you can give climbing plants in pots. These make ideal presents for friends with small yards or with no walls suitable for climbers. Training the growing shoots around the frame will give the present a continuing interest, especially for those who love gardening and clearing things up! You can buy containers specially for growing climbing plants with supports built in, like the baskets shown on the right, or you can purchase frames of different shapes and sizes to insert into pots. It is also easy to make your own simple supports from bamboo stakes or from flexible twigs such as hazel or willow.

Many climbing annuals can be easily grown from seed: try nasturtiums, sweet peas, black-eyed Susan, and morning glory. If choosing perennials try plumbago, passion flowers, and the less rampant types of honeysuckle. Grow seedlings of annual climbers in small pots; transplant them when big enough into the larger, decorative container and pinch out the tips of young plants to encourage branching. Or check out the local garden center for interesting small climbers to buy.

Try to choose a frame which will be right for the eventual size of the plant and sturdy enough to support it without looking too obtrusive. When putting a frame into a container, make sure it is firmly anchored in the soil and that it will not fall out when the plant gets bigger and heavier.

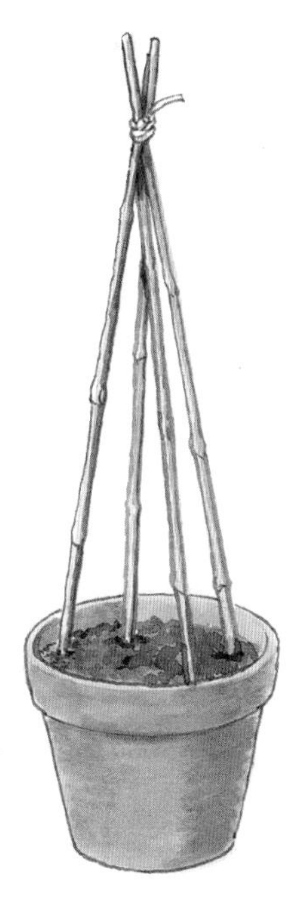

Left: The annual climber black-eyed Susan grows well in a pot supported by stakes. This container looks great in a sheltered spot on a patio or low wall, or it can be put in a border to add height and interest. To ensure your present stays flourishing, give a copy of the care notes on page 125. For ideas on making decorative tags to tie on your container, see page 114.

Above right: There are many attractive types of garden containers with supports built in. These can be used year after year, with new plants put in each spring. These basket containers are best suited to miniature nasturtiums and sweet peas, but you can buy large containers with trellis or decorative wooden frames attached for climbers such as clematis or honeysuckle.

Above: Bamboo stakes pushed into a large pot and tied together at the top with garden string or wire will support a summer-flowering annual. Plant four or five seedlings in the pot to provide a good display of flowers.

Hostas

Hostas fall into that useful category of plants that come up by themselves every year and can be easily divided to make more plants – so they are perfect to keep on hand as an instantly available and inexpensive green gift. Moreover they offer great beauty of shape and texture. The leaf colors, both plain and variegated, range through green, gold, silver, and blue according to variety; while the foxglovelike flowers, though not spectacular, are an added interest in summer. Some are even scented. The biggest problem with this plant is keeping the leaves undamaged, since to slugs and snails they seem to taste like strawberries and cream! Growing them in pots is some deterrent, but be sure to give a copy of the care notes on page 125 with your gift.

When planting bought or divided hostas in a pot, choose a container that will allow for the plant to increase in size. Use a soil-based potting mix and make sure there is good drainage by putting a layer of stones or gravel in the bottom of the pot. Feeding and topdressing (scraping off soil and putting on a fresh layer of soil mixed with fertilizer) are important for good growth and flowering. Look for other hardy perennials that grow well in pots. You can enjoy them for several years and then give them as gifts whenever you choose.

DIVIDING HOSTAS

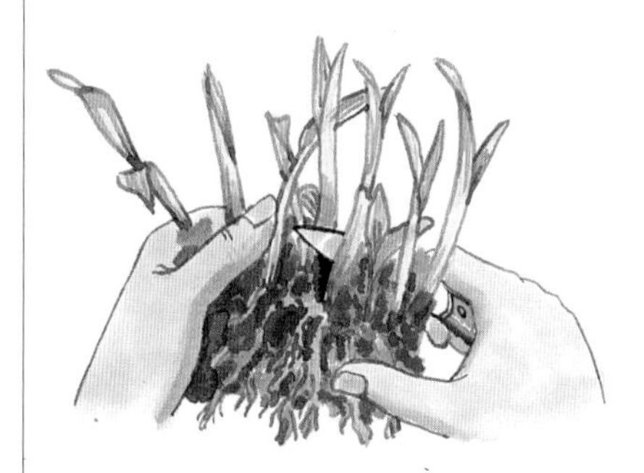

1 Divide hostas in the spring. Large hostas with tough roots may need to be divided with a spade. Smaller clumps can be pulled or cut apart. Make sure there are several buds or shoots on each division. Cut away any damaged roots or leaves.

2 Plant the divided sections as soon as possible. Put them in a pot with plenty of stones or gravel at the bottom to provide drainage and use good quality soil-based potting medium. Spread the roots out well and firm in. Water the pot well.

Left: This group of hostas displays the appealing variety of leaf form and color offered by this versatile plant. Hostas prefer moist, shady conditions; they also tolerate polluted air so are good for urban yards shaded by the surrounding houses. Their leaves can be used to great effect in flower arrangements – as shown on page 44.

Above: The rather severe architectural quality of hostas usually appears to best advantage in a natural-colored pot. But if you want to try something more adventurous than terracotta pots for your hostas, see the instructions on page 119 for decorating pots with pebbles or shells for a mosaic effect.

OTHER HARDY PERENNIALS FOR POTS

Agapanthus
Heathers
Bearded Iris
Hellebores
Day Lilies

Summer posies

Above: A selection of pretty posies picked from the summer garden uses flowers, grasses, foliage, and berries in simple but charming combinations. Glass jars decorated with ribbons make ideal containers for these "cottage garden" posies.

There is a charm about uncontrived posies of garden flowers that often wins over the more formal arrangements available from florists. Sometimes the limitations of choice force you to be more experimental: try wandering around the yard picking a flower here, some foliage there, with no particular design in mind. In no time at all you will be holding a delightful posy.

Top right: A sophisticated-looking posy with a subtle color scheme has some surprising ingredients – leek flower heads from the vegetable patch and variegated hosta leaves from the flowerbed are combined with cow parsley from the roadside and eucalyptus from the florist. This is a good example of how you can use materials from a variety of sources.

Center right: A late summer posy makes use of the ripening berries of the guelder rose, Viburnum opulus, combined with white achillea flowers and the leathery leaves of the senecio shrub with their silvery margins. A hopsacking bow echoes the color of the berries.

Bottom right: This cool yellow and green posy is a mixture of lemon yellow chrysanthemums and hypericum berries from the florist, and flowers and foliage from the summer flowerbed. The flowers have been placed on a large castor oil plant leaf and tied with ivy around the stems.

Posies are lovely, unpretentious little presents and are suitable for many occasions: the birth of a baby or a fragrant reminder of the natural world for someone who is ill. Even the smallest backyard can be a source of flowers and foliage because they are needed in such small quantities – a single rose, some trailing ivy, a few sprigs of lavender, and a hosta leaf, and you have the makings of a posy – even wildflowers such as campion and buttercup can be incorporated. And if your yard is really bare, there should be no problem in finding a few stems at the florist to complete your posy.

Left: There is no need to limit your palette when gathering a summer posy – in the garden there are very few colors which don't look good together, and on a miniature scale, this glorious mixture of colorful flowers is reminiscent of the herbaceous border in high summer.

Below right: Who can resist a scented posy? Here fragrant sweet peas in shades of red, pink, and purple are mixed with aromatic lavender to make a posy that will fill a room with its heady scent.

It is always best to cut summer flowers early in the day, preferably before the sun is fully on them; flowers picked later will have lost some of their moisture and are more likely to wilt. As soon as possible after picking, stand the flowers in cool, deep water for at least three hours to condition them. Once flowers are properly conditioned, they will last well.

Tie the stems of your posy together using green garden twine or dark cotton thread – a decorative ribbon or bow can then be added at the last minute to make sure the ribbon stays looking crisp. Or decorate the stems with a twist of ivy. The posy can be assembled some hours before it is needed and kept in a cool place. Small posies can even be kept in the fridge, although it is best to check them for insects beforehand!

One of the great advantages of garden posies is that they are ready to be popped into a vase, but bear in mind that your hosts may be too busy to stop and look for a suitable container, so either take one with you as part of the gift or wrap the stems in moist sphagnum moss. This will keep the flowers fresh for some time. Transporting the posy in a glass jar means the stems are in water and gives the posy a temporary home on your arrival. Indeed, the home need not be temporary, as a recycled glass jar can look appealing in its own right.

TOP TEN FLOWERS FOR SUMMER POSIES

Roses
Sweet Peas
Lavender
Nasturtiums
Marigolds
Phlox
Astrantia
Pinks
Clematis
Achillea

TOP TEN FOLIAGE PLANTS FOR SUMMER POSIES

Ivy
Rosemary
Hostas
Ferns
Grasses
Sage
Alchemilla
Artemesia
Mint
Scented Geranium

Lilies

In striking contrast to the riotous colors of summer annuals, lilies have a serene and stately appearance which will please anyone who loves flowers. They grow very well in containers, given a rich, but well-drained soil and can be happy in a semi-shaded position. A cool place indoors will also be suitable for some types, such as the Easter lily, which is half hardy. Several have the added bonus of a wonderful perfume.

Although there are many different sorts of lilies, the newer hybrids such as the Asiatics are more tolerant of varying conditions and therefore the easiest for the beginner to try. There are plenty of colors and various shapes of flowers to choose from. Many people love the splendor of the white regal lily, and these are also quite easy to grow in a pot. Make sure you buy plump, fresh-looking bulbs and don't let them dry out. Plant them in the fall as soon as possible after purchase: three to a 10-inch pot is about right. Use stoneware or terracotta pots, but not plastic, which will get too hot for the roots. Put a layer of sand under the bulbs to ensure they do not rot, keep them cool (but frostfree) and not too wet while starting to grow. Once they have made good shoots, water frequently.

Above: One advantage of having lilies in pots is that you can give them the type of soil that they like, which you cannot always do in garden soil. Mix in some rotted manure or garden humus to give extra nourishment. This will produce good flowers over a longer period. For care notes to give with your lily pot see page 125. For information on painting and decorating pots, see page 118.

Left: Lilies make stunning cut flowers, too. These are displayed with hosta leaves.

Right: If you didn't plant lily bulbs in the fall, you should be able to find a good selection of plants to buy in garden centers during the summer. Put two or three plants together in a lovely pot and plant some small annuals around the stems. The lilies shown here are partnered by white daisies. Don't forget to put a copy of the care notes on page 125 with your gift.

Right: A wooden wheelbarrow makes an attractive and unusual container for tomatoes, cucumbers, decorative lettuce, and herbs. The barrow can be filled with bulbs in the fall when the vegetables are over. Be sure to give the care notes on page 125 with your gift.

Left: Sweet peppers are ideal subjects for containers if they are grown in a well-sheltered, sunny spot, and should produce a fine crop in late summer. This pot contains an unusual marker made from a small ceramic pepper glued to a wooden rod. If you enjoy giving green gifts, you will want to keep an eye out for horticultural "accessories", such as greetings cards featuring beautiful gardens, fridge magnets made in the shape of flowers, and toy snails, bees, and butterflies to stick on pots, plants, and tags. The photograph on page 110 features a host of possibilities!

Vegetables

Even the smallest cucumber tastes better if you have grown it yourself. Your friends can enjoy the pleasure of homegrown vegetables without the effort when you give them containers planted with, for instance, young tomatoes, lettuces, and zucchini. Growing vegetables in containers is also an excellent way of introducing children to the fun of gardening – they can eat the results!

Not all vegetables are suitable for container growing, either because they don't look attractive or because the growing conditions are not right, but there are plenty that can be successful. Concentrate on the fast-maturing sorts and avoid those which get very big such as broccoli. Salad crops, such as lettuce, scallions, outdoor cucumbers, and beet, do well, while zucchini and beans have the bonus of very pretty flowers. Your aim should be to make the container look as attractive as possible throughout the season, so choose lettuces with curly or red leaves and tomatoes with yellow or striped fruits.

The container itself should be deep and wide enough that the plants do not dry out and have room to develop. Remember that root vegetables especially go down as well as up! Various types of materials and

shapes can be used effectively, from painted window-boxes to wooden half barrels and even hanging baskets. Smaller pots can be used for plants such as radishes and lettuces, perhaps as a single crop planting.

The soil needs to be fertile and well drained, so use a rich potting mix with added granular general fertilizer and put plenty of drainage material in the bottom of the container. Mix in well-rotted manure or garden humus if possible. It is best to plant the container with small plants you have grown from seed or bought at the garden center – although some quick growers such as radishes can be sown directly into the container.

VEGETABLES FOR CONTAINERS

Beans

Beet
globe varieties

Carrots
early varieties

Cucumbers
outdoor varieties

Eggplants

Zucchini

Lettuce
cut-and-come-again or small-headed varieties

Radishes

Scallions

Sweet Peppers

Tomatoes
small-fruited bushy or trailing varieties

Houseplants

SUMMER-FLOWERING HOUSEPLANTS

- **Achimines** *(cupid's bower)*
- **Pelargonium** *(geranium)*
- **Begonia**
- **Gloxinia**
- **Impatiens**
- **Italian Bellflower**
- **Black-eyed Susan**
- **Chinese Hibiscus**
- **African Violets**
- **Cape Primrose**

Right: An arrangement of houseplants makes a memorable gift. Here, African violets and Cape primroses are grouped together to great effect. For information on making tags, see page 114. For care notes for summer houseplants, see page 125.

Below: Giving two plants in matching pots turns a simple gift into something much more special.

If you have a yard of your own, it is easy to forget that a housebound relative or a city apartment-dweller will be delighted with a gift of flowering houseplants. To lift your gift out of the ordinary, select the plant with care and put it in an attractive pot. If you can afford to, give a group of plants that look good together. A small display is more eye-catching than a single plant.

Choose plants which have healthy foliage and are just coming into flower, with more buds developing. Unless they are very young, or are really over-filling their pots, it is best not to replant them into your chosen container, which could disturb the roots and affect the flowering. Just make sure the new container is large enough to hold the pot the plant is in. If there is room, put gravel in the bottom of the new container to assist drainage and fill any gaps with more gravel, covering the top of the soil as well. This will help keep a humid atmosphere around the leaves, which is especially important indoors in summer.

Two of the best long-flowering plants to give are African violets (*Saintpaulias*) and Cape primroses (*Streptocarpus*), both of which come in shades of pinks, mauve, and white. Both plants can also be propagated from leaf cuttings. For the African violet, cut off a whole leaf together with a section of the stalk. Push the stalk (keeping the base of the leaf above the soil) into a small pot of cutting medium. The stalk should then form roots. A Cape primrose leaf needs to be divided horizontally through the central vein and both halves inserted, cut side down, into a pot of cutting compost. Put the pot in a clear plastic bag and keep shaded. Small plantlets should develop along the vein.

Herb wreath

Midsummer, when herbs seem to grow faster than you can pick them, is a time to be generous with their bounty. Moreover, when herbs are in full growth, they really benefit from regular harvesting; it encourages the production of fresh young shoots and delays flowering. Like most other plants, once a herb plant has flowers, it concentrates on setting seed rather than sending up new growth, so frequent picking will benefit both you and the plants.

A herb wreath is both a visual and an olfactory delight and has the advantage of being useful as well as decorative – what more could you ask of a gift? This is the perfect present to take along to a summer dinner party: so much more original than a bunch of flowers and ready to be hung on the wall or to be used as a centerpiece on the table.

To make a herb wreath you will need a circular wire frame, sphagnum moss, mossing wire, garden twine, scissors, and bunches of your chosen herbs. Pick the herbs and put them in separate containers of water while you work. For detailed instructions on how to make a wreath, see page 97. If you don't have time to make a whole wreath, you can still give little bunches of herbs tied with ribbon or raffia (see the photograph on page 123). They smell great in the kitchen or in the car!

Some herbs are better suited to use in a wreath than others: sage, rosemary, thyme, bay, lavender, origanum, and marjoram will stay fresh longer and dry well, whereas herbs such as chervil, cilantro, basil, and sorrel quickly wilt and fade. If the herbs are destined to be used for cooking, it is best to hang the wreath away from direct sunlight in a cool position. This will ensure that the herbs retain their aromatic qualities.

Above and left: A moss-covered ring is the base for a garland of fresh herbs. Variegated sages, bay leaves, rosemary, and lavender combine in a fragrant display that can be used as a purely decorative object or as a source of fresh, then dry herbs. Make herb wreaths on a "one for me, one for you" basis – if you only make one, you won't want to give it away, and it is far quicker to make extra wreaths when you have all the materials at hand.

Pots of color

Summer is the time for lots of exuberant, bright colors in the garden. An easy way to achieve this is by filling decorative pots with bedding plants which will flower all season. The choice of flowers is enormous, and you can achieve spectacular results either from seeds sown yourself early in the year or from young plants bought at the garden center. Be adventurous and try some of the newer, less common plants that are now available. Many of these are really tender perennials, such as osteospermums, Swan River daisies, and margaritas, but are used as annuals for beds and containers. They mix well with the tried and tested favorites such as petunias, marigolds, and pansies. Geraniums and fuchsias are, of course, wonderful for continuous color and can be grown among smaller plants such as lobelia or sweet alyssum.

The container itself should be very much part of the whole arrangement, preferably in a striking color to complement the flowers. Pots and windowboxes can be painted to give the desired effect (see page 118 for instructions). But think carefully about the overall color scheme and don't use too many different colors in one container.

Use a good potting medium when planting and put plenty of drainage material at the base of the pot. Use enough plants to give the container an "overflowing" effect. However, you mustn't squash in the roots or they won't develop well. Make sure all the plants are properly hardened off and starting to come into flower before giving your present away.

Above: The dark green of background ivy throws the exciting colors of this group of summer pots into prominence. Added interest comes from the use of an old watering can as a container. Put a lot of stones or gravel in the bottom if there are no drainage holes.

Right: Different levels increase the impact of these brightly colored pots of pelargoniums (geraniums). They have been placed outdoors so they blend into the surrounding flowers and foliage. Be sure to give a copy of the care notes on page 126 with your gift if it is going to less experienced gardeners! And remind them that pots can be used to fill a gap in the flowerbed as well as a feature in their own right.

Above: Be unconventional! Here, a plastic shopping bag has been turned into a fun summer container. A present for a gardener with a sense of humor! This one has been packed with pansies, nasturtiums, heather, and trailing ivy.

Right: A more conventional planting has been made in this interesting wirework trough – ideal for displaying on a garden table. Or attach a chain or rope to the handle to turn it into a hanging basket. The basket is planted with three different varieties of bellflower.

Right: The terracotta of these wall plaques and pots looks great against this brick wall – their matching textures and tones contrasting with the brilliant colors of the flowers. Remember plants in wall containers need shelter from cold winds and very frequent watering. Try adding water-holding polymers to the potting.

A large container full of summer flowers is probably a gift best given to someone you know well. Then you will have an idea of where the container is likely to stand. Most summer annuals do best in a sunny position, sheltered from wind, but there are those such as impatiens and lobelia which will be happy with a fair amount of shade – their colors will last longer and they can brighten up a dull corner. Pots in shade also have the advantage of not drying out so quickly.

The background against which the arrangement will be seen can play an important part in the overall effect. Local stone or brick used for the house and in the yard may not complement every container. In the same way, remember to consider the standing ground. Concrete will not be much of a problem, but gravels vary quite a bit, as do patio paving stones, and brightly painted containers will need to tone in with their bases.

Standing the planted pots against some foliage, such as dark evergreens, can enhance the colors of the flowers as well as adding some life to a shrub which is otherwise uninteresting.

Take care getting your carefully prepared container to its lucky recipient. You don't want all your work to be ruined if the pot falls over when your car goes around a corner! Stand the pot in a large box and wedge it securely with crumpled newspaper.

SUMMER-FLOWERING PLANTS FOR CONTAINERS

Antirrhinum
Asteriscus
Begonias
Candytuft
Convolvulus
Dahlias
Felicia
Fuchsias
Geraniums
Margaritas
Marigolds
Nemesia
Pansies
Petunias
Verbena

Strawberry pots

Above: If growing plants are not a suitable gift, you can still give strawberries. Select some really fresh fruits and clean and wash them if necessary. Line a pretty basket with a colorful napkin and arrange the fruit inside. Take a gift like this along to a summer picnic or party, and everyone can help themselves!

Fresh-picked strawberries have a flavor all their own. Grown in a bed in the garden they take up lots of space and need a good deal of care, but they can also be produced successfully in containers and make a delicious gift. Not only will the plants give an enjoyable crop of fruit, but there will also be flowers which are pretty and decorative, so there is a long season of interest. Your friend may even be able to reciprocate with a jar of home-made strawberry jelly!

Containers must be of a size to hold enough plants to give a reasonable crop. The traditional terracotta or stoneware "strawberry pot" with side planting pockets, is the best, but can be expensive to buy. There are various plastic alternatives available based on the same principle, or you can use a large wooden, pottery, or terracotta container. A flat-bottomed basket or painted wooden trough makes a very attractive holder for several small pots of individual plants, especially if you use pretty little Alpine strawberries.

Use a soil-based medium in the container for greater stability and take care that there is good drainage by putting plenty of gravel or stones in the bottom of the pot. (For detailed instructions on planting a strawberry pot, see page 29.) Late summer or fall is the best time for starting this project since the plants can then become established during the winter (make sure they don't get waterlogged) before you give

them away the following year. If possible present your gift when the strawberry plants are coming into flower: not only will they look attractive, but the plants will be settled in their new home by the time the fruit is forming and ripening.

If you can provide some form of protection, such as a cold greenhouse, early in the year, the strawberries will flower and fruit sooner than usual.

Above: The very well-organized can plant their strawberry pots in the fall ready to give the following year. The less well-prepared can buy plants at the garden center. Choose varieties that will grow well in a pot and be sure to give a copy of the care notes on page 126 with your delicious gift.

Topiary

Traditional topiary is on a grand scale – amazing shapes cut into large hedges in country-house gardens. But you can achieve a similar effect on a small scale by growing twining plants around ready-made metal frames and clipping them to shape. These make expensive-looking presents which can be displayed indoors or out. If the topiary is to go outside all year round, make sure you use hardy plants. Lots of different topiary shapers can be found in garden centers. Don't be too ambitious at first: choose something relatively simple and not too big, taking care the frame is balanced by the size of the container.

Foliage plants are best to use for this form of topiary as they can be shaped without fear of removing developing flowers. Ivies are ideal as they are tough, grow quickly, and have hundreds of variations of leaf shape and coloration. When planting, put the frame in first, well anchored, and then put several small plants around it, pushing the stems up into the shape and twining them around the wires. Encourage strong growth by regular liquid feeding and allow the shoots to fill in the frame before attempting to snip too much off. However, pinching off the tips will help branching and promote vigorous growth.

Right: Look for a frame to suit the interests and personality of the person you intend to present with your topiary masterpiece. You can either give it soon after planting so the recipient looks after its future development, or keep it until the frame is covered (see the care notes on page 126).

Left: You can give a topiary gift at almost any time of the year, but be careful to choose hardy plants if it is to live outside all year round. And be sure to give the care notes on page 126 with your gift. For information on making decorative tags, see page 114.

FALL

As leaves turn color and drift down from the trees, there is a harvest of gifts just waiting to be gathered.

Fall ideas

One moment you are revelling in the dry, dusty heat of high summer and the next a leaf swirls down and you know that fall has arrived. There is inevitable sadness at the end of summer, but who can really regret the arrival of fall with its gloriously colored foliage, misty mornings and ripening fruit?

This is a time of harvest and as you gather herbs and flower heads for drying, and fruit and vegetables to preserve and store, there will be many opportunities to transform your more abundant crops into green gifts. Lavender harvested in late summer and hung up to dry will be ready for making into fragrant lavender bags or to be used as an ingredient in potpourri. Hydrangea flower heads and other flowers and foliage such as yarrow, fennel, sunflowers, and poppy seedheads can be hung up to dry for displays that will last all winter.

Fruit trees often seem to operate on an all-or-nothing basis: in a "nothing" year each fruit is precious, but in an "all" year, the crop can seem endless even after you have bottled, frozen, and dried for days on end! The obvious solution is to be generous and give your surplus away, but, instead of simply filling paper bags, arrange the fruit in pretty rustic baskets and add ribbons or a handmade gift tag. This will transform

Left top to bottom: The end of summer does not mean that there are no more green gifts to give until the spring. On the contrary: dried flowers such as lavender make charming gifts turned into traditional lavender bottles or sewn into sachets. And there are plants, such as ornamental cabbages, which will brave the cold.

your surplus into a much-appreciated gift, ideal for harvest, Halloween, and Thanksgiving parties.

This is the time to replant your own windowboxes and pots with flowers and foliage that will last through to the spring. While you are doing this, plant some extra containers to give away as gifts. Choose the contents carefully and they will last until spring. Fall is also the right time to buy bulbs. Friends and relatives with yards will appreciate a gift of bulbs, especially if you package them prettily and include decorative containers and labels, while friends without a yard can be given gifts of forced bulbs to flower indoors.

As winter draws nearer cut flowers become more and more expensive to give as gifts, so this is the time of year to give houseplants instead. Put them into a decorative pot or basket and conceal the soil with moss or gravel to give them a special finish. Don't forget to consider cacti – they make great gifts for friends who don't have green fingers.

Make your own labels and tags in place of the ones that came with the plant – the cultivation and care instructions look far nicer when handwritten. At this time of year you can also make your labels look appropriately seasonal with brightly colored leaves, nuts, or berries gathered on autumnal walks in the woods. Nature's fall bounty can also be used to make wreaths, table decorations, and embellishments for parcels and packages. Gather some especially beautiful fall leaves and berries to press or to gild for use at Christmas.

Right top to bottom: Fall provides great free gifts in the shape of beautifully colored leaves and a harvest of interesting nuts and berries. And if you are looking for presents to buy at the florist or garden center, there are lots of plants which will flourish indoors to give as gifts. Make them special by adding tags and handwritten care notes or by putting them in a new pot.

Lavender

The soothing scent of lavender on a hot day is one of the joys of summer. This delightful fragrance can be captured to bring back warm memories on cold winter days – making dried lavender a welcome gift, whether in bunches, in potpourri, in a pretty sachet, or woven into a striking wreath.

Lavender is easy to grow provided you have a sunny spot and a well-drained soil. If your soil is not suitable or you don't have room, you can grow lavender plants in a container (especially the smaller forms). A decorative pot with a lavender plant inside makes a great gift in its own right. There are lots of different varieties to choose from, although some are hardier than others and some are stronger in fragrance (see the list on page 66).

The colors of the flowers vary from white through pink to mauves and purples, making them highly decorative outdoors as well as useful. Most varieties grow to between 1 and 2 feet high. Plants should be lightly trimmed in late spring and after flowering in late summer. Never cut hard into the old wood as the plant may not recover.

Above: You can make a sweet-smelling wreath very easily. Buy a decorative wreath base – the one pictured here has twig binding, but you can wind thick string or ribbon around it. Tie up little bunches of dried lavender and tuck them into the wreath under the binding. Wire them in place if necessary. If you wish you can tuck other dried leaves, flowers, or berries into the wreath.

Far left: Use the heart template on page 121 to make lavender sachets. Cut out two fabric hearts using pinking shears. Stitch them together, leaving a small gap to insert the dried lavender. Close the gap and decorate with buttons. No-sew lavender bags are even quicker to make – and children can join in, too. Cut circles of fabric, put lavender in the center, then gather up the edges, and tie with ribbon. To make a summer potpourri, mix about 2 ounces of dried lavender with roughly equal amounts of the following dried ingredients: rose petals, marigold heads, blue delphinium petals, lemon verbena leaves, and eucalyptus leaves. Add 1 ounce of powdered orris root and a few drops of geranium oil.

Left: You can give lavender in many different ways and they will all smell wonderful! The twig hearts are made by bending flexible Y-shaped twigs downward and tying to make a heart shape.

HOW TO MAKE LAVENDER BOTTLES

It is best to pick lavender for making bottles when the stems are still green and flexible. Otherwise, they may break when you bend them over. You will need 15 stems of lavender for each bottle and about three yards of narrow ribbon.

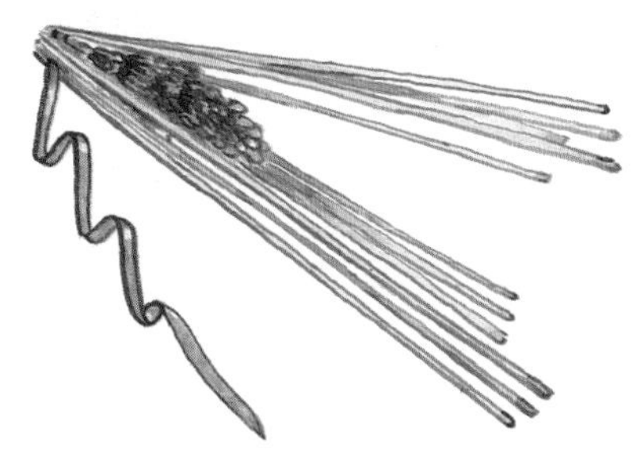

1 Put the stalks together so the heads are at the same height. Tie narrow ribbon around the stems just below the heads. Leave one end of the ribbon long. Carefully, one at at time, bend the stems back on themselves to enclose the heads.

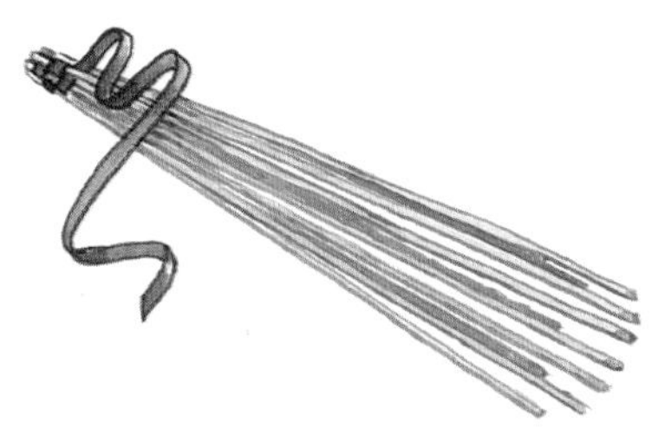

2 Pull the long piece of ribbon to the outside. Weave it over one stalk and under the next. Continue until the heads are enclosed. If you want to change ribbons, tie the new piece to the end of the old, making sure the knot is concealed inside the bottle.

3 Fasten the end of the last piece of ribbon by tying it around a stalk and pushing the knot and end to the inside. Cut the stems even and tie decorative ribbons around them. The lavender is now safely enclosed, and cannot shed petals, while the delicious lavender fragrance can still be smelled.

You can get free lavender plants by taking cuttings of shoots in summer and rooting them in potting mix under shaded glass. Use soil specially designed for cuttings. When they have grown on, these make good presents or replacements for your own plants.

Lavender flowers should be harvested as they begin to open. Choose a dry day in summer and lay the flowers on paper to dry indoors, out of the sun.

Above: Use the heart template on page 121 to make this sachet. Cut two hearts and sew with right sides together. Leave a small gap to turn the hearts right side out and fill with lavender. Sew up the hole and decorate with buttons.

Right: A collection of lavender bottles tied with differently colored ribbon makes a very special present. These certainly deserve to be displayed, not hidden in the linen closet! For ideas on making gift tags see page 114.

VARIETIES FOR COLOR AND SCENT (all hardy)

English Lavender - *purple*

Hidcote - *violet*

Hidcote Giant - *purple, tall flower spikes*

Royal Purple - *deep purple, retains color well after drying*

Folgate - *violet-blue, good scent and free-flowering*

Munstead - *pale lavender-blue, strong scent*

Imperial Gem - *deep purple, good for hedges, fragrant*

Hidcote Pink, Loddon Pink, Rosea - *all pink flowers*

Nana Alba - *white, compact*

Alba - *white, long flowering season*

Alpines

Alpines (or rock garden plants) can be used to make a miniature outdoor garden which will give years of pleasure to someone with little space for bigger plants. Most alpines stay small but come in a huge variety of forms and produce exquisite flowers. Your local garden center should have a good selection.

Alpines can be presented in a small container which the recipient can put on an outdoor table or window-ledge. The container can then easily be moved into a more sheltered spot in bad weather. Wooden containers must be lined with thick plastic, with holes made for drainage. Plastic containers are best avoided for alpines. If you want to make a larger display in a stone sink or other large container, add one or two interesting rocky stones, partly buried, in the top before planting your selection of alpines.

The main point to remember when giving rock plants is that true alpines come from mountainous regions, so they need conditions which are open and dry rather than humid and wet. They do not mind being exposed to wind but don't like wet soil. Drainage is extremely important to prevent the roots from rotting,

Above left: A small wooden basket makes a perfect home for dianthus, wood sorrel (*oxalis*), houseleeks, saxifrage, and hardy cyclamen.

Above: Rock plants perching on and inside two birdhouses make an original and eye-catching display. The plants used are gentian, miniature iris, and dwarf hypericum in the blue birdhouse, and diascia and dianthus in the checkered one.

so make sure the container you choose has drainage holes (drill them if necessary), and put at least 1 in of gravel or stones at the bottom. Fill the container with a mixture of soil and peat and at least one third sand.

Put the clump-forming plants towards the center of the container and trailing sorts around the edges. Cover any bare soil with grit. Water the plants well and allow them to settle for a week before giving your gift. Be sure to include a copy of the care notes on page 126. These will help the recipient to keep your gift looking great.

DWARF AND COMPACT ALPINES FOR CONTAINERS

Alyssum - *yellow*

Dianthus - *pink, red, or white*

Gentian - *blue or white*

Houseleek - *yellow, pink, or mauve*

Rock Jasmine (*Androsace*) - *pink*

Rock Rose - *white, yellow, orange, pink, or red*

Saxifrage - *white, yellow, pink, red, or mauve*

Sedum - *white, yellow, or pink*

Harvest inspiration

Golden autumnal days, when the air is warm but the shadows are long, mean leisurely walks are a delight. Everything seems touched with gold, as if to highlight the value of these last days before we turn more to indoor activities during the winter months in cold parts of the country.

Although most of us no longer need to be involved in the harvest for our survival, harvesting is a natural instinct, and it is fun to celebrate the season by gathering some of its bounty to decorate our homes and those of our friends. Fallen leaves, twigs, bark, cones, nuts, mosses, and berries are all around and can provide the materials for many green gifts. It is important to remember that some of the items you may gather provide food and shelter for wild creatures. Never take more than you need. You should also be aware that in certain areas, such as protected woodland and nature reserves, and on private land, you are not allowed to remove anything at all.

Your own yard can be a rich source of materials: flowerbeds can be full of seedheads at this time of year; St. John's wort has glossy rust-colored fruits which darken to matt black; ivy berries nestle in the glossy foliage, and the leaves of some shrubs are as dramatically colored as their woodland counterparts. Clearing up the garden can be combined with harvesting all sorts of natural materials.

Left: Terracotta pots filled with damp floral foam hold candles surrounded by ivy leaves and berries, sprigs of heather, oak leaves, and acorns. See page 102 for detailed instructions and note the safety warning.

Right top to bottom: Set the scene for autumnal celebrations such as Halloween and Thanksgiving with an appropriate table centerpiece. Gourds, nuts, or a decorated candle will all look appealing.

Much of the harvest is so decorative that all you need to do is to assemble a still-life as a seasonal gift. Fill a basket with sweet chestnuts gathered as the glossy brown nuts begin to burst from their prickly carapaces: their color, texture, and shape need no further embellishment. Windfall apples, with all their imperfections, look wonderful piled high in a glass bowl. Crimson, vermilion, and saffron yellow leaves pressed under a sheet of glass are as bold and vivid as an Impressionist painting. When you look closely you will be amazed at the beauty of nature's harvest.

Left: A bark box is given a finishing touch with a cluster of dried hawthorn berries, while its oval companion is overflowing with a fragrant fall potpourri. Make a 1-pound mixture of acorns, dried rosehips, horse chestnuts, bay leaves, bark, moss, and dried oak leaves. Add 1 ounce of ground cloves and 1 ounce of powdered orris root plus a few drops of cedarwood oil. The miniature wreath is studded with seedheads.

Below: Tie little bunches of colorful fall leaves to decorate your gifts.

Many of the fruits of the harvest are ideal to use as ingredients in an autumnal or woodland potpourri – leaves, mosses, berries, nuts, and cones can be scented with spices and woody essential oils, matured, and then packed into plastic bags to give away as aromatic gifts. Nuts, seedheads, and pods glued onto small foam rings make decorative wreaths. If you use horse chestnuts, they will soon lose their glossy shine and become dull and wrinkled; this, too, has its charm, but it is less obvious. Keep a supply of leaves, twigs and berries on hand to decorate gift tags and presents.

PRESSING LEAVES AND GILDING

As the fall begins to fade and leaves, seeds and berries no longer look so attractive, you may want to press and gild some items to keep them looking great right into the Christmas season.

1 Choose a selection of leaf shapes – thick leaves such as oak, bay, and aucuba are best since they tend to be less brittle. Arrange them between sheets of newspaper and press with a heavy weight Leave for several days.

2 Spread the pressed leaves out on a sheet of newspaper in a well-ventilated room or work outdoors. Spray each leaf evenly with gold paint, holding the can at least 8 inches away from the leaf. Gold paint is available in a variety of shades – vary the finish on different leaves to add interest.

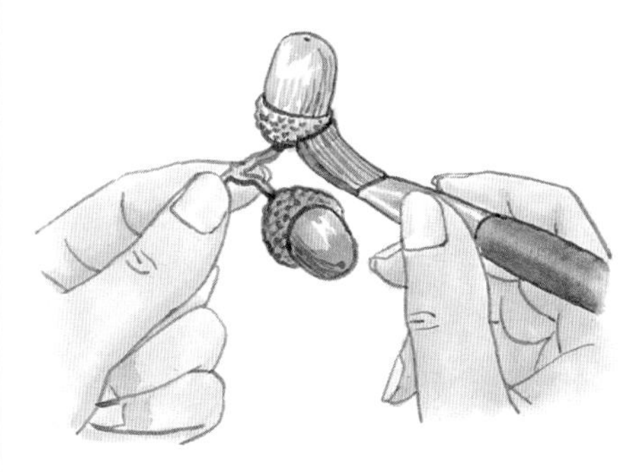

3 To decorate acorns and other nuts apply, liquid gold paint with a craft paintbrush. Make sure they are completely dry before attaching them to tags or using them to decorate presents.

Desert cacti

Cacti are the ideal gift for friends who travel a lot or lead very busy lives. Cacti require little care but look extremely stylish. They come in a wide range of shapes – columnar, round, jointed, and flat, or fingerlike and trailing. The spines form many variations, too: some are very prickly (handle with care!), others have long, hooked spines or a mass of soft wooly "hair". By using a number of different varieties, you can create interest and texture within your design – either by putting different cacti together in one container or by giving a group of plants to display together.

Choose an attractive bowl for a desert garden, bearing in mind that the sides will probably not be covered by trailing leaves. The bowl can be shallow as the roots are not deep. Drainage holes are not absolutely necessary, although if there are none it is best to put a thicker layer of gravel and charcoal on the bottom and be extra careful not to overwater. The potting medium must be very free-draining, so add one part of coarse sand to two parts of soil-based medium.

Before actually planting the cacti, arrange them in the container to get the best effect. Bring the soil just to the base of the swollen stem so that the cactus appears to be sitting on the top of the soil. Leave a gap around the rim of the bowl so that you can finish off with a layer of tiny chips of gravel or small pebbles. For a more decorative effect use colored glass pebbles. Be sure to give a copy of the care notes on page 126 with your gift.

HOW TO TRANSPLANT PRICKLY CACTI

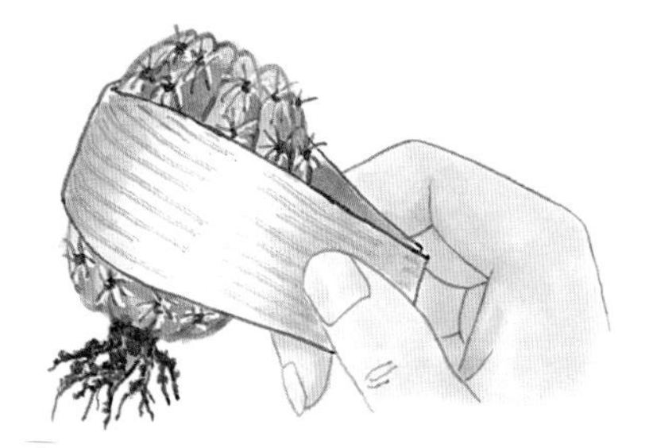

1 First loosen the cactus in its pot by pushing a pencil up through the drainage hole. Take a strip of thick paper and use it as a handle to lift the cactus out. If the roots are very squashed, loosen the soil around them.

2 Put the cactus in its new pot. If you are repotting to give the plant more room, choose a pot only one size larger.

Above left: If you use small stones to cover the surface of the soil, you may like to continue the theme and use tiny pebbles, stones, or shells to make a gift tag for your present. For ideas on making decorative tags, see page 114.

Right: A display of different shapes and sizes of cacti in carefully selected containers can look stunning. Cacti can live in a sunny spot outdoors during summer and then be brought indoors when it gets cold.

Above: Choose bright pots to bring color to cool fall and winter days. This orange windowbox is planted with ornamental cabbages, variegated ivy, curry plants and heather. If some plants, survive the cold and others do not, you can put in replacements. Give a copy of the care notes on page 126 to help the recipient look after the gift.

Right and far right: Ornamental cabbages can look extremely striking planted together in a container. Choose varieties with different colored leaves for a really entertaining effect. This amusing gift will bring a smile to the lips of anyone who sees it.

Windowboxes & pots

Outdoor containers can be planted in the fall to give color and interest well into the winter months. You can choose from a range of plants for a windowbox or a pot which will tolerate, and in some cases even enjoy, a cold climate. Study the list on the right for ideas.

One of the more recently available and spectacular plants for fall is the amusing ornamental cabbage, or brassica, which has leaves in shades of blue-green, red, purple, cream, or white that actually brighten in color as the temperature drops. Raise them from seed sown in the summer (try Osaka or Tokyo varieties) or buy young plants from garden centers.

Ornamental cabbages combine well with winter-flowering heathers, which have similar coloring and, unlike most heathers, do not require lime-free soil. Winter pansies are another favorite, although they need to be in a sheltered position if they are to continue flowering right through the winter.

Given some protection from cold winds and rain, you can try some late-flowering houseplants such as cyclamen or cinerarias. They need to get used to outside conditions gradually, but as they prefer cool conditions to a centrally heated room, they may well survive for some weeks, especially if not allowed to get too wet.

You will need some foliage to act as a foil and fill in the gaps. There are plenty of evergreen variegated and colored leaved plants available, both upright and trailing. Ivy is an obvious choice, with many different varieties both in leaf shape and color. Shrubby herbs, such as rosemary or the curry plant, can also look very effective with their gray, spiky needles. Many evergreens, such as low-growing cotoneasters, have berries as well, but watch out as these may be taken by birds if they are not protected.

PLANTS FOR FALL CONTAINERS

Ornamental Cabbage - *for bright colored leaves*

Summer/fall-flowering Heathers - *soil must be lime-free*

Winter-flowering Heathers

Pansies - *colorful flowers*

Polyanthus - *colorful flowers*

Cyclamen - *pink, red and white flowers*

Cinerarias - *blue, red, and white flowers*

Trailing Ivy

Curry Plant - *gray foliage*

Rosemary - *gray-green foliage*

Cotoneaster - *red or pink berries*

Holly (female) - *foliage and berries*

Hebe - *gray or variegated foliage*

Euonymous - *variegated foliage*

Conifers (dwarf) - *colored foliage*

Left and below left: Colorful heathers are a great fall and winter standby. They look good on their own or mixed with other plants. If you want to give just one plant, make it special by putting it in a colorful pot – see the instructions on page 118 for painting and decorating pots. For original tags to hang on your gift, see page 114. Winter-flowering heathers do not need a lime-free soil so they can be grown in any ordinary potting mixture. Flower colors range through white, various shades of pink, and red. The blooms last for many weeks and also make very good cut flowers. Plants should be trimmed lightly after flowering. Some varieties also have golden or bronze foliage.

Right: Cyclamen are usually bought as house-plants but may do better out of doors since central heating will make them shoot up and fade very quickly. Their flowers are very attractive, and plants are easy to find in florists and garden centers in the fall. Cyclamen kept indoors need a cool, moist atmosphere with good light but not direct sunlight. They should be stood in a tray of wet pebbles and the leaves misted regularly. Water from below the pot (stand in a saucer of water for about half an hour, then remove) to avoid overwatering.

You can leave shrubby evergreens in their pots when putting them in a windowbox or other container. They are then easily removed at the end of the season. The pots can be buried in earth in the flowerbed for the summer and brought back into use the following fall.

When planting the containers make sure there is plenty of drainage material at the base and in the potting soil, since too much water will cause damage to roots. It is a good idea to give some of the terracotta "feet" available from garden centers with your fall gift so the box or pot is kept off the cold, wet ground. Alternatively, provide a few bricks or large flat stones for it to stand on. Try to see that there are no overhanging roofs from which rain or melting snow can cascade onto the container below. Give a copy of the care notes on page 126 to help the recipient keep your gift flourishing.

Hydrangeas

Hydrangeas give a superb show in late summer and fall, and as an additional bonus, the flower heads can be cut and dried. Those plants most commonly grown in containers are called mopheads (round) or lacecaps (flat) according to the shape of the flower heads. Flowers vary from creamy white through shades of pink and mauve to blue. You can alter the color of pink varieties yourself by adding a commercial "blueing" agent to the soil in the container.

Hydrangeas are not difficult to grow, and they will keep flowering for years given reasonable attention. They can be treated as outdoor plants or as indoor ones, providing they are kept cool and moist. Correct pruning is essential as this group flowers on growth made the previous year, so over enthusiastic cutting at the wrong time can lose next year's flowers. Check out the care notes on page 126. As this should be a long-lived plant, use a soil-based rather than peat-based potting medium in the container and make sure it is ericaceous (lime-free) if you want blue flowers. Choose a pot that allows for root growth, especially if it is to stand outside, and keep it well watered at all times except in winter.

Above: Hydrangeas can live for many years in a pot. Regular liquid feeding in the growing season will produce plenty of flowers. Protect the roots and the new shoots from frost. Put the pot in a sheltered spot and wrap it with sacking or garden fleece when hard frosts are forecast. Be sure to give the care notes on page 126 with your gift to make sure it has a long life.

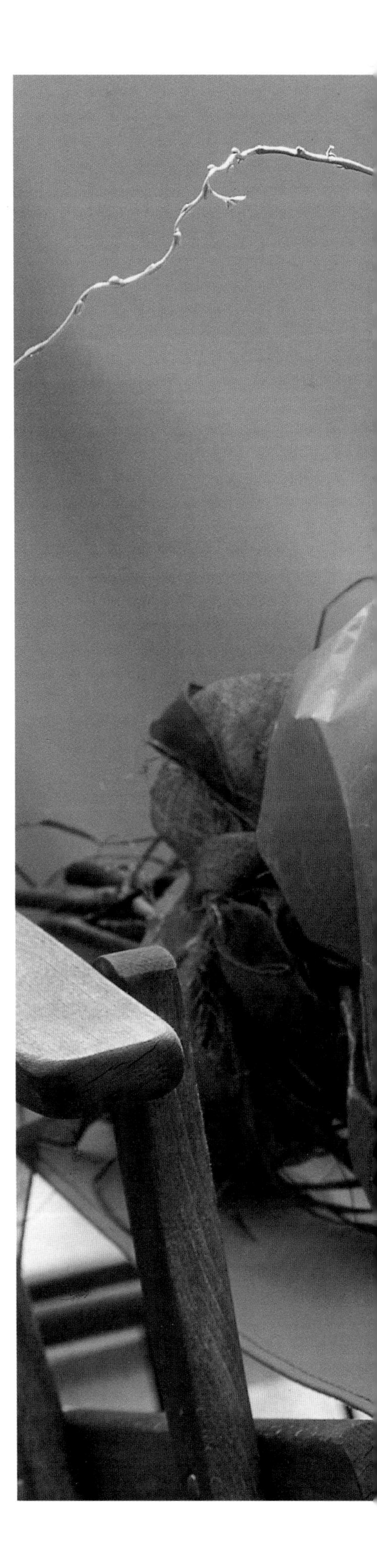

Right: Flowers can be cut for drying when they are fully open. Do not pick them when they are wet with rain or dew. Remove the leaves. Air drying is the easiest way to preserve the flower heads: hang each head upside down separately (so they are not touching) in a warm, dry shed or spare bedroom. Keep them out of direct sunshine. Leave until they feel crisp and dry.

Left: Baskets of rosy, crisp apples decorated with bunches of berries and leaves capture the very essence of fall. This is a great gift to take along to a Thanksgiving dinner.

Right: Fig leaves add an exotic touch to these velvety purple plums, which should be picked and eaten as soon as they are ripe. A basket like this is a perfect dessert at the end of an fall supper or lunch party.

The rich color and texture of fall fruits in a basket makes a perfect gift at this time of year. You can combine any garden produce such as apples, pears, and plums together, or put them separately with foliage to soften the arrangement. Soft fruits, such as fall strawberries or blackberries, are best on their own so that they are not damaged by other fruit. Soft fruits also need to be given away as soon as they are picked, for they will not store well.

Apples are the most successfully stored fruit, but only the mid- or late- season varieties will keep for any length of time. If you have a glut, it is worth storing some to give later in the year. Ideally each one should be wrapped individually, but if this is not possible, put them into large plastic bags left open at the top. The idea is to stop the apples from shriveling, so they also need to be kept in a cool, moist atmosphere such as an outdoor shed or garage which is frostproof. The fruits must be sound with no disease or bruising – and should be examined regularly for possible rotting.

Pears will keep indoors provided they are not in a centrally heated room, unless of course you want them to ripen quickly. They do not need to be wrapped, but lay them on trays or shelves so they do not touch. Ripening is often very quick, so keep an eye on them! Plums do not really store very well, but they can be kept for a few days if picked a little under-ripe and put in a cool, dark place.

Don't forget that fresh, scrubbed vegetables can also make a very interesting and attractive fall display. Don't worry if you don't grow your own produce: vegetables and fruit bought from the supermarket still make an unusual gift if you present them wrapped in a napkin or arranged in a pretty basket or bowl.

Indoor garden

As flowers outdoors fade, indoor plants become increasingly important. Choose the right plants to give and they will provide interest and pleasure right through the winter months. Arranging a group of plants together in an attractive container will provide not only an interesting display but also a better environment for them, especially if you can stand the pots on a tray of wet gravel. Central heating and drafts are a problem for houseplants in winter, but the most common source of trouble is actually overwatering. Even foliage plants which stay green all winter need a period of rest: the aim should be to keep them alive without expecting active growth. Hence the need for less water and less feeding and, usually, a cooler temperature. The exception to this is those plants that are still in bloom, such as African violets. Giving a copy of the care notes on page 126 with your gift will help the recipient keep the plants flourishing.

Foliage plants that have tough leaves, such as the Swiss cheese plant or mother-in-law's tongue, are the easiest to keep in good condition, and small plants can be bought at a reasonable price. There is a wide choice of other plants available, many of which have variegated or colored leaves. However, beware of those that look too exotic since they will be more difficult to keep healthy. Most flowering plants are not usually long-lasting at this time of year, although the winter cherry and indoor heathers can be if they are kept cool and are misted with water frequently.

Above: The bright orange berries of the winter cherry add a splash of color to foliage plant groupings.

Right: Polka-dot plants need plenty of bright light to keep their pink spotted leaves from turning green. Pinch out flowers and young shoots to keep them bushy.

Above left: For ideas on making tags and greetings cards to go with your gift, see page 114.

PLANTS FOR INDOOR DISPLAY

TRAILING HABIT	UPRIGHT HABIT
Swedish Ivy *(Plectranthus)*	Sweetheart Plant (*Philodendron*)
Ivy *(Hedera)*	Rubber Plant
Wandering Jew (*Tradescantia*)	Weeping Fig
	Fatsia
BUSHY HABIT	Fatshedera
Aluminum Plant	Dragon Tree
Peperomia	
Polka-dot Plant	

Bulbs to grow

Dry and brown they may be, but a gift of bulbs brings a promise of spring which will delight any gardener. Imaginative packaging is really important here, and the addition of some accessories, such as a bowl and a small bag of potting medium, can turn a few bulbs into a more substantial gift. There are lots of different bulbous plants to choose from: for the more experienced gardener look for something unusual such as dwarf iris or winter aconites. Buy from a garden center or by mail order, but make sure the bulbs are firm, disease-free, and generally of good quality. Cheap ones are only useful for naturalizing in grass or under trees. September and October are the best months for planting, although November is fine for planting tulips.

There are different types of bulbs available to buy. Forced bulbs are intended for indoor flowering as early as possible – usually for Christmas. These bulbs must be bought specially "prepared" and will be labeled as such. You should find hyacinths, narcissus, daffodils, and tulips. The bulbs will need a period of cool and dark, followed by warmth and light (see page 127 for care notes to give with forced bulbs).

Ordinary bulbs can be given for the recipient to plant outdoors – in containers or in the garden. Bulbs in suitable containers can be brought indoors when the flower buds appear. For care notes to give with these bulbs, see page 127. If you want to plant containers yourself to give in the spring, see page 104.

For bulbs that will give an informal effect planted in grass or under trees, give narcissus types as well as scillas, grape hyacinths, crocus, or tulips.

Above: One bulb can make an amusing gift. Tie a tag around it (see page 114 for tag ideas) to make it special. Giving one bulb per person means you can afford to present a whole group of people with a little autumnal gift.

Right: A gift of bulbs can be presented in a variety of appealing ways. Put the bulbs in a decorated paper or fabric bag or in a gift box or plant them in a pot ready to grow. Be sure to give a copy of the relevant care instructions from page 127 with your gift. Bulbs make a good gift for a child – in which case it is best to give the potting medium and pot with the bulbs. The child can then have the satisfaction of planting the bulbs and seeing them flower in the spring.

WINTER

When it is cold and unwelcoming outside, bring the beauty of the countryside indoors for your family and friends.

Winter ideas

As the old year gives way to the new, many people take time to renew ties with their family and friends. This usually involves an exchange of gifts – and what better gifts to give than those which will continue to give pleasure long after all the parties are over! Attractive and amusing containers planted with bulbs, fragrant flowers, and houseplants will all continue to flourish into the spring. Some will continue to grow for years to come given the right care and attention.

Seasonal decorations made with natural materials also make great green gifts. They may not last as long as a growing plant, but a beautifully decorated wreath or Christmas tree will bring pleasure to everyone who sees it. When brought along to a family gathering or party, the appreciative audience will make all your efforts worthwhile. In many homes the Christmas tree is the focal point of the celebrations, but not all homes have space for a full-size tree, and not everyone has enough time or money to buy and decorate one. So a miniature tree, already decorated, can make a great gift. Hand-made decorations, using simple natural materials, have a unique charm – every one is individual. A little fir tree hung with aromatic dried oranges looks wonderful on a side table in an entrance hall or as the centerpiece on a

Left top to bottom: No matter what the weather is like outside, there is always a green gift to be given. Even bare twigs can be given a starring role with a little skill and imagination! If you didn't plant bulbs in the fall don't despair: florists and garden centers will have plenty to buy. You can put them into eye-catching containers to make wonderful presents.

festive table. The fragrance of the oranges will fill the room, and if the care notes on page 127 are followed, the tree should survive to ornament another Christmas.

The Scandinavian tradition of hanging a wreath on the front door to welcome visitors is now universal: an undressed door looks bare at this time of year. Wreaths can be made well ahead of the holiday and kept in a cool place until needed. While you are making your own wreath, it will not take much longer to make one or two extras to give away. Pine, fir, and other evergreens can all be used to make wreaths and other seasonal decorations. Gilded leaves and berries will add a touch of glamour.

Flowering bulbs are always a welcome gift, especially when they are imaginatively planted in a container which complements the flowers. Rustic twigs tied with raffia or sisal string can be used to support the flowers and foliage and will add to the overall effect. For non-gardeners there are some bulbs which do not even require soil to grow: forced paperwhite narcissus will grow in a glass bowl filled with gravel, and a hyacinth bulb need only have its base touching water to flower and fill a room with scent.

Novelty containers planted with foliage plants make great presents and are especially appropriate for children who are just beginning to take an interest in growing things. They are also great gifts for children to make themselves and give to friends and family. If you are looking for a more sophisticated present, choose scented houseplants, such as jasmine, gardenia, or stephanotis. They will fill a room with their fragrance and make a luxurious and lasting green gift.

Right top to bottom: There is a green gift for every occasion, every age group, and every member of the family. And there are green gifts that are just right for work colleagues, neighbors, and friends near and far. From fun flowerpot faces with hair that grows to wreaths and miniature Christmas trees, this is a season to give green: even the tree angel can be given green wings!

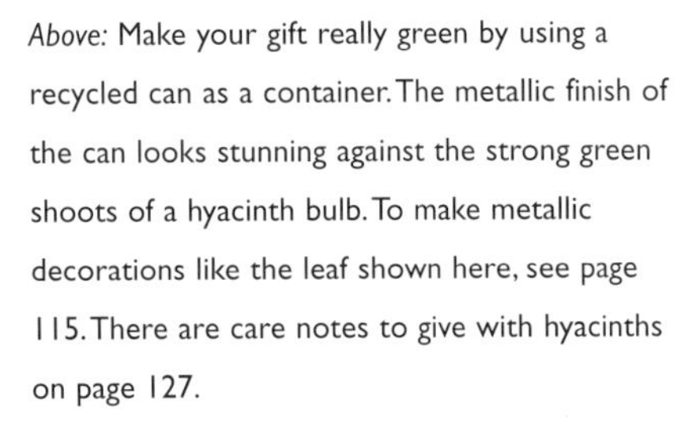

Above: Make your gift really green by using a recycled can as a container. The metallic finish of the can looks stunning against the strong green shoots of a hyacinth bulb. To make metallic decorations like the leaf shown here, see page 115. There are care notes to give with hyacinths on page 127.

Right: A collection of containers makes a really eye-catching and unusual display. Alongside the cans, water glasses have been pressed into service with the bulbs suspended on twig platforms.

Hyacinths

The scent of even a single hyacinth flower in a room is remarkable. From Christmas on through the early months of the year, their exotic perfume drives away the gloom of winter, making them the perfect gift for cheering up a friend or colleague. The flowers are usually delicate shades of pink, blue, creamy yellow, or white, although there are varieties that are red or dark blue. Hyacinths look good in all sorts and shapes of containers and will even grow without soil provided the base of the bulb is in water.

Hyacinth bulbs are easy to grow. Plant them in the fall using ordinary plastic flowerpots (see the care notes on page 127 for planting bulbs), then transfer them to more interesting and exciting containers when the buds begin to show and they are ready to give away. If you haven't had time to grow your own hyacinths, there will be a plentiful supply in shops and garden centers that you can repackage in just the same way.

Another way to grow a hyacinth is in a glass that has been made to hold the bulb above a column of water. The base of the bulb should just touch the water. The roots will grow down the length of the glass making an interesting pattern, while the flowering shoot is produced above.

In addition to the usual single-headed hyacinths, there are also multiflora types that can be grown indoors. They have looser flower spikes, several to each bulb, and are deliciously scented like the traditional ones.

Wreaths

Above: A festive wreath richly decorated with berries, fruits, and cones is a generous gift for anyone with a busy life struggling to prepare for the holiday season. A colorful gift tag can convey your message with the gift. For ideas and instructions on making tags, see page 114.

Far right: This sophisticated and stylish wreath is decorated with lichen-encrusted twigs. These have been bound to the moss-covered frame using garden twine. Some of the moss has been allowed to show through to complement the lichen. Sprays of red and black berries add color and contrast to the overall design.

Right: Gray lichen has been glued to a foam ring to make a wreath which looks good in the stark simplicity of a very modern home or office. The splash of color provided by the gift tags gives its austerity a festive touch. For instructions on making tags, see page 114.

The traditional homemade wreath with holly, pine, and berries is a relic of our pagan past when evergreens were brought indoors to symbolize continuing life. Nowadays the festive door wreath has become a symbol of a home ready for celebration, where a warm welcome is assured. When you make your wreath, make another for a busy neighbor. Such a thoughtful and unique gift is sure to please.

A simple moss-covered ring is the starting point for all sorts of beautiful wreaths. Materials gathered from the backyard, hedge and even the supermarket shelves can all be pressed into service. Decide on your theme and gather your materials together before you start working – it is very frustrating to decide that your finishing touch will be sprigs of holly berries, only to discover that the birds have beaten you to it and there are no berries left!

Wire frames for mossing are available from florists and garden centers in several sizes, or you can make your own ring. Use heavy-gauge garden wire or bend two coathangers into a circle and bind them together with wire or string. Sphagnum moss for filling the frame can be bought from the same sources and should be used moist for wreaths that feature fresh foliage, berries, and fruit. Detailed instructions for making a wreath are given on page 97.

CREATING A WREATH

To make a wreath you will need a circular wire frame; sphagnum moss; green garden twine or mossing wire; stub wires; evergreen foliage; a selection of twigs, cones, berries, or fruit for finishing touches; scissors and glue gun (optional).

1 Pack damp moss firmly into the topside of the wire frame. Hold it in place by looping mossing wire or twine around the frame. Make a hanging loop at the back.

2 Prepare small bundles of foliage tied with twine or wire. Working consistently in one direction, fasten the bundles to the moss ring. Do this by looping twine or wire around the ring and then around the stem of the bundle. Make sure the head of each bundle overlaps the base of the previous bundle.

3 To fasten items such as crab apples to the wreath, push stub wire through the fruit, bend it back on itself and twist. Push the stub wire all the way through the moss ring from front to back, bend at right angles and fasten to the frame. Small cones and pods can be glued in place.

Before you begin work on a wreath, prepare a good supply of foliage bundles. If you have to keep stopping and starting, it will hinder the rhythm of your work, which can make the result less satisfactory. Work in one direction around the wreath, overlapping the bundles as you fasten them in place. Don't neglect the side of the wreath – otherwise, it may look lovely from above but bare and bitty at the sides. To check, bend down and view it from the side as you work. The final decorative flourishes of cones, berries, or fruit should be added once the moss ring is fully covered by foliage. They can be wired or glued in place; you may find a glue gun useful.

Left: A fruit- and berry-encrusted Christmas wreath is a feast for the eyes. Sprigs of deep green yew, with their attractive silvery undersides, have been tied into bundles and fastened to the moss-covered frame. Crab apples, berries, and cones add color and texture while sprigs of holly and ivy complete the picture.

Above: Blue pine is a lovely material to work with: its color, shape, and texture are unrivaled and it is wonderfully fragrant. On this wreath it has been combined with sprigs of myrtle and clusters of eucalyptus pods. Lichen-covered twigs have been inserted at random to break the outline of the wreath.

Left: A plain pot has been turned into a face by the clever addition of a clay nose and eyebrows. If your sculpting skills are not up to this, try painting or gluing on the features. An ornamental cabbage makes a startling hairpiece!

Flower-pot faces

An amusing and memorable way to give a houseplant is to turn it into a hair plant! It is not difficult to give an ordinary plain container a "face". Then put a plant in the pot for "hair" which really grows. You can achieve a sophisticated look with cacti hair and masklike features, or you can let the children loose to paint and glue funny faces which will amuse their friends and be proudly displayed by Grandma!

It is best to choose plants with either a trailing or spiky habit of growth for "hair". Buy houseplants grown for their leaves rather than for their flowers. The size of pot and plant must be well balanced so that neither overwhelms the other and so that the face is clearly visible – you may need to do a little trimming with some plants. The head looks most effective if the foliage comes directly from the rim of the pot, without a bare stem making a gap.

Most flowerpot faces will be used as indoor decorations and placed on shelves and tables to be admired at close hand. However, you can also adapt the idea for growing herbs such as parsley, where the "hair" is snipped as required for cooking. The pots should then be somewhat larger in size and stood either in the kitchen or outdoors on the patio. Children will also enjoy planting chives or mint in their flowerpot faces and waiting for edible hair to grow.

PLANTS FOR "HAIR"

- **Cacti** - *round, wooly or trailing forms*
- **Succulents** - *rosette forms*
- **Ferns** - *small-leaved, feathery forms*
- **Grasses and sedges**
- **Creeping Fig**
- **Swedish Ivy**
- **Creeping Moss** *(Selaginella)*
- **Mind-your-own-business** *(Helxine)*
- **Ivy** *(small leaved)*
- **Peperomia** *(trailing forms)*
- **Spider Plant** *(Chlorophytum)*

Above: Two tropical-style pots proudly display hair made from a variegated trailing fig and tufted grass respectively. To make pots like these, look for small stones, pebbles, or pieces of broken china or tile. Then glue appropriately shaped pieces to a flowerpot to make eyes, nose, ears, and mouth. If you choose a pot with handles, you can make matching earrings by winding wire around stones and suspending them from the handles.

Left: This crazy character has cactus hair and shell, glass, and stone features. The metal pot gives him a very stylish, modern air. Add interest by winding wire around some of the stones and glass before gluing them firmly in place.

Christmas

More and more people are turning away from the tinsel and baubles of the commercial Christmas and once again enjoying a "green" holiday. A living tree, decorated with simple homemade decorations, is a welcome relief after all the glitter, and with the right care the tree will survive the year to be enjoyed again next Christmas.

You are most likely to keep a Christmas tree alive if you buy a pot-grown tree; a bare-rooted tree has often been lifted weeks before and may not survive, however much loving care you give it. While the tree is indoors, keep it as cool as possible and position it well away from radiators or fires. Keep the soil moist at all times and mist the foliage occasionally if you can do so without damaging the decorations. Alternatively you can spray the tree with unscented hair spray before you bring it indoors. This cuts down on evaporation through the needles and washes off when the tree is returned outdoors. After Christmas the tree needs to be put in a shady spot outside where it will not dry out, or planted in the ground.

If you cannot find a tiny living tree to give, there are many alternatives available that look good with natural decorations. An ivy-twined moss topiary tree should continue growing after Christmas (see page 58 for topiary ideas). Or for a natural look, without the responsibility of a growing plant, buy ornamental trees made from dried twigs or branches.

Left top to bottom: Use pine cones and other natural decorations to continue a green theme. Cones can be used as table decorations or given as little gifts – this one has a fabric star stuck into it (use the template on page 120). Dried oranges make fragrant tree decorations. For instructions for making them, see page 102. For a dove template see page 121.

Right: Three little Christmas trees – each one a perfect and unusual gift or centerpiece. The growing tree is decorated with dried oranges. The twig tree has been filled with moss, and horse chestnuts have been glued between the branches. The topiary tree is made from a wire-netting cone stuffed with moss. The ivy planted in the pot is being trained around the wire.

HOW TO MAKE A CANDLE DECORATION

Candles in decorated pots are a great gift at all times of year (see the summer candles at the bottom of page 35 and the fall candles on page 70). You will need a flowerpot; candle; green floral foam; paring knife; foliage, flowers and berries.

1 Decorate the pot if you want to (see page 118 for ideas). Soak the foam until it is pliable. Cut it roughly to shape and push into the flowerpot. Trim away excess foam. Position the candle in the center of the foam and push it into place.

2 Arrange the foliage around the candle, fanning it out and away from the base. Include some trailing greenery which will hang over the edge of the pot.

3 Add the flowers and berries and other finishing touches such as gilded leaves (see page 73 for information on gilding).
It is important to use only wet foam as dry foam could catch fire. Never leave a burning candle unattended.

To make dried orange decorations, use thin-skinned, medium-sized oranges and slash through the skins from top to bottom, evenly around the fruit. Place them on a rack above a cookie sheet in a low oven for a few hours until the skin has hardened. Open the oven at regular intervals to check on progress and to allow moisture to escape. Complete the drying process on a radiator. After 10 days the oranges should be fully dried. Twist thin wire around them to form a cage, add other decorations if you wish, and hang from the tree or use a wreath.

Above: Simple but striking natural wreaths can be made by attaching dried and gilded leaves (see page 73) to twig wreath bases (see page 97). A striking star can be made from twigs tied together. Use small versions to tie on the tree.

Right: A candle makes a great table centerpiece to take to a dinner party or use yourself. Buy a few sprays of flowers at the florist and add bits and pieces from the yard or field.

Bulbs in flower

In the midst of dreary winter weather, flowering bulbs give a wonderful lift to the spirits. Some, such as hyacinths (see page 92), have the added bonus of scent. If you have been organized and planted bulbs in the fall to give as gifts in the winter and early spring, you will now be a very popular person! If you were not that farsighted, you can still put together some highly original green gifts. Check out the local florist and garden center. If you buy bulbs in boring plastic pots, they will not be too expensive. Replanted in decorative containers with moss added around the base and decorative twigs for supports, they will look stunning. Hyacinths and daffodils, grown from bulbs which have been specially treated before purchase, can be ready as Christmas presents. And a bowl or basket of bulbs ready to flower is a great gift even for friends whose houseplants rarely survive! Bulbs are easy to look after. All the "food" is already within the bulb, so water and some advice on positioning is all that is required.

To have bulbs for display indoors flowering earlier than they would outside, the bulbs must go through a period of cool and dark to develop roots and shoots. Always choose good-quality bulbs (look for ones which have been specially prepared for forcing if you want to give bulbs in flower for Christmas or New Year celebrations) and plant them in bowls of bulb fiber. Keep the fiber moist (but not soggy). Leave the bulbs in the dark for 8 to 14 weeks. When shoots begin to show

Above: Snowdrops or crocuses potted up from the garden can be brought inside for everyone to enjoy the flowers. Arrange them in a container such as this shallow basket, covering the edges of the pots with moss and adding twigs for support and decoration.

BULBS FOR WINTER FLOWERING

- Daffodils and Narcissus
- Hyacinths
- Tulips
- Crocus
- Grape Hyacinth
- Dwarf Iris
- Snowdrops
- Scillas

Left: Grape hyacinths give a heartwarming display of brilliant blue flowers. These have been planted with the bulbs close together and just sitting in a little depression in the growing medium. Keep a gift like this in a cool place until it is time for it to be presented.

Right: One flower ornaments a tag to go with your gift (see page 114 for more tag ideas).

bring them into the light but keep them in a cool place for a while. Turn the bowls regularly to keep the growth from bending toward the light. Try not to get water on the leaves. If you want a gift for a particular time, perhaps as a birthday present, the development of the flowers can be hastened or retarded by the temperature at which they are kept. For instance, if the bulbs seem to be growing too quickly, put the bowl into the coolest place in the house, or even somewhere outside provided it is frost-free, and then bring it into the warmth a few days before the birthday celebrations to encourage flowering.

To achieve a really color-packed display in a big container, perhaps for a feature outside the front door or in a large room, plant bulbs such as daffodils at two levels. Space them so that there is room for each shoot to grow straight up. They should all flower at the same time and give a wonderful show.

With most bulbs, once flowering is over, the bowls should be put into a cool place and kept watered until the foliage dies down naturally. A liquid feed with the watering at this stage will improve the flowering for next year in the ground, but do not try to grow the same bulbs again for display indoors. Once the leaves have withered, the bulbs can be dried off and planted outside in the late summer.

PLANTING BULBS

Plant bulbs in the fall to give early the following year. Plant some for yourself and some to give away.

Plant daffodils about as far below the surface as the height of the bulb. Make sure there are plenty of stones or some gravel in the bottom of the pot to aid drainage.

If you are planting a large pot, try making two layers of bulbs. Check that the shoots of the ones below won't hit the bulbs above when they start growing. The bulbs should all flower at the same time.

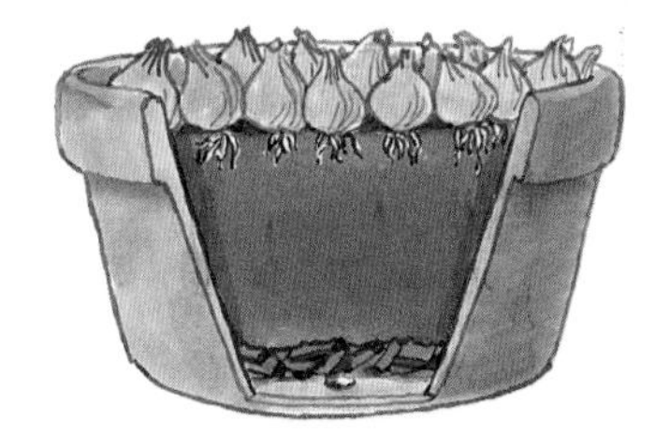

To achieve an effect like the grape hyacinths shown on the left, use a shallow bowl. Put stones or gravel in the bottom, then fill with bulb fiber. For each bulb make a little depression in the top of the soil. Cover with black plastic and put in a cool, dark place until the shoots appear.

Left: The semi-double, scented blooms of gardenias and their dark, glossy leaves make a luxurious-looking gift, especially when well presented. They need special care to keep healthy, with particular attention to steady warmth and high humidity – standing the pot on wet pebbles is helpful. Care notes to give with gardenias are given on page 127.

Right: Jasmine and stephanotis are displayed in metal pots decorated with raffia bows. The plants have both been trained around simple wire hoops to give them added interest. Care notes to give with jasmine and with stephanotis are given on page 127.

Scented houseplants

Houseplants are often given as gifts, but presenting a sweet-smelling, flowering plant in a stylish pot makes the gift a special treat – especially if it is cold and wet outside and no other plants are in flower. Jasmine and stephanotis are ideal houseplants to give in the winter. Jasmine is an easy, vigorous grower producing masses of delicate-looking white clusters tinged with pink. Stephanotis is a little more difficult but is worth the trouble, having exotic, waxy flowers and thick, shiny leaves. Both are strongly and sweetly perfumed.

An added attraction is that they have twining stems that can be trained into interesting shapes over a framework. Buy the plants when young (cuttings are not very easy to root, so propagating your own is not recommended) and you can make your own individual design using hoops of bent wire or wickerwork pushed into the soil. After buying, unfasten the stems from any sticks already attached to them. Twist the shoots around

your chosen frame, tying in the shoots with twine or small metal split rings. Be careful not to tie them too tightly as this will restrict the growth. You can also try training around other shapes such as fans or rectangles. Maintaining the form of the plant by careful pruning after flowering is over will be part of the pleasure given by the gift, as it should last several years with reasonable care. Be sure to give a copy of the care notes on page 127 with your present.

OTHER WINTER-FLOWERING HOUSEPLANTS

Azalea
Poinsettia
Cyclamen
Chrysanthemum
Cineraria

FINISHING TOUCHES

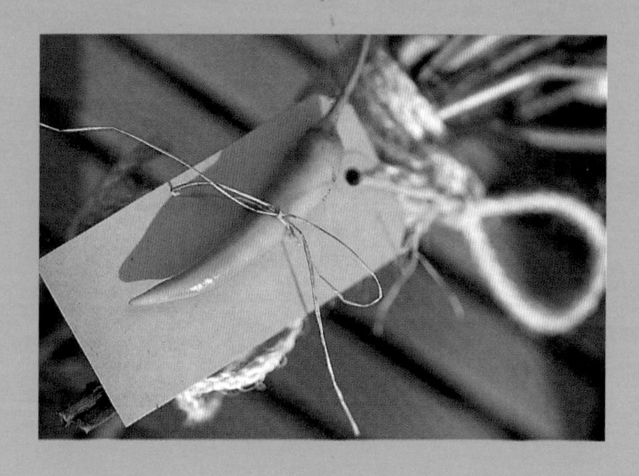

Find out how to make those all-important finishing touches that will make your green gifts really special.

Wrapping flowers and pots

Above: One small plant wrapped in brightly colored paper tied with a bow makes a great little gift. Tuck in a matching homemade tag (see page 114) or a tiny bunch of berries, leaves, or flowerheads for the perfect finishing touch.

It takes very little time to wrap a bunch of flowers or a pot plant in an individual way, and this little extra effort will make your gift really memorable – whether it is a bunch of flowers bought from a florist or a plant you have grown yourself. Brightly colored tissue paper looks stunning with strong-colored flowers such as gerbera or tulips. Be careful not to get tissue paper wet as water marks it easily and the colors may run. Put wet flower stems or damp pots in a plastic bag before wrapping with paper. For a more substantial wrapping, useful if you have to carry your gift some distance, put flowers or pots in strong brown or colored paper lined with tissue. For a really original look use scissors or a decorative hole punch to cut holes in the plain outer paper so the tissue shows through.

Other green gifts can also be lifted out of the ordinary with clever packaging. Design your own seed packs for a little gift with a lot of potential (see page 18). This is an ideal project for children, and the finished gift can be mailed to friends far away. A collection of small plants such as herbs can be put in matching pots – or even in brown paper bags (see page 28). Pretty baskets lined with colorful napkins are very appealing filled with fresh fruit or scrubbed vegetables (see page 56). A gift of fall bulbs looks good in a decorated cloth or paper bag (see page 87).

Above: Bunches of flowers – fresh or dried – can be given a "special occasion" look with a unique wrapping. See the steps opposite for how to achieve this effect. If you don't have a decorative hole punch to stamp out hearts or similar patterns, you can give the paper a decorative edge by cutting a scalloped or zig-zag pattern along the top.

Right: A purchased pot of flowers can be given a luxury look by wrapping it in brown paper lined with tissue paper.

WRAPPING FLOWERS

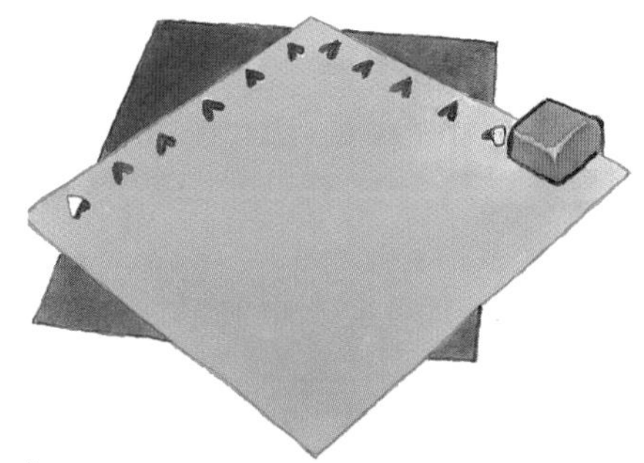

1 Measure the height of the flowers you want to wrap. Cut a piece of wrapping paper and a piece of colored tissue paper to the same height and about third again as long. Punch or cut holes along the top edge and down one side of the wrapping paper.

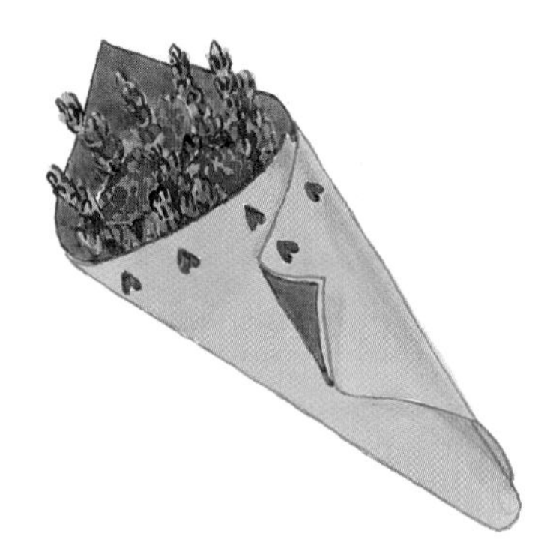

2 Put the tissue inside the wrapping paper and place the flowers in the center, heads pointing to one corner. Roll the paper into a cone shape, keeping the point at the top. Secure it with tape and decorate it with a tie and a tag.

WRAPPING POTS

Line a large square of brown or other strong paper with contrasting tissue paper. Put the pot in the middle with one corner of the papers pointing up. Wrap the paper around the pot, making sure the tissue shows. Secure with tape, then tie with raffia or ribbon.

Gift tags and decorations

Left: These seed packs have been decorated with wire and tissue motifs. For instructions detailing how to make these, see page 116. Many more of the decorative ideas shown here for making tags can also be used on colored envelopes to create gift packs for seeds.

Above: Look out for stamps featuring appropriate gardening motifs such as butterflies or bees. Simply stamp your tag and use it on your gift. If you have more time, stamp the motif onto a separate piece of contrasting colored paper, cut it out, and then glue it to the tag. Little pictures cut from magazines or seed catalogs can be used in the same way. For a 3D effect use foam mounts to attach the motif: this will give it a raised appearance.

A handmade tag to carry your message of love, congratulations, or good wishes will add style to the simplest gift. You can also write out or photocopy and glue the relevant care notes (see page 124) onto a large decorated label to give with your green gift. And a little tag can be turned into a striking greetings card if you glue it to heavy paper or cardboard (see page 117).

Use the luggage label shapes or one of the other motifs such as the heart on page 121 as a template to make a tag base or cut your own base shape. Use thin cardboard and punch a hole in the top to thread with ribbon or string. There are hundreds of ways to decorate your tag. If you are going to attach something bulky to the front, such as leaves or twigs, it is best to write your message on the back first.

Above and below: For a special, shiny effect, buy rolls of thin silver, gold or copper foil (see right) and cut out shapes such as leaves or flower heads. Add details of veins and petals by drawing on the back of the metal with a ballpoint pen. These decorations can be glued to cardboard to make tags and greetings cards.

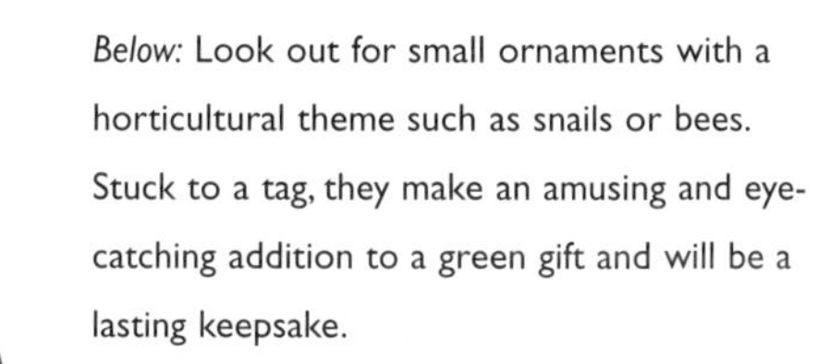

Below: Look out for small ornaments with a horticultural theme such as snails or bees. Stuck to a tag, they make an amusing and eye-catching addition to a green gift and will be a lasting keepsake.

METALLIC TAGS

You can buy thin sheets of aluminium foil in craft stores. These sheets are thin enough to be cut with an ordinary pair of scissors. Aluminum cans can be cut in the same way. The potentially sharp edges means this is not a suitable project for children.

1 Cut a cardboard template for the shape you want. There is a selection of leaf templates to choose from on page 121. Cut a small piece of foil, place the template on top, and draw around it using a sharp pencil.

2 Cut out the shape carefully using sharp scissors.

3 On the back of the foil shape draw in details such as veins on a leaf. Use a ballpoint pen to make the indentations.

MAKING A WIRE AND TISSUE TAG

These unusual decorations are best made with the sort of thin, flexible wire available from florists for wiring plant stems.

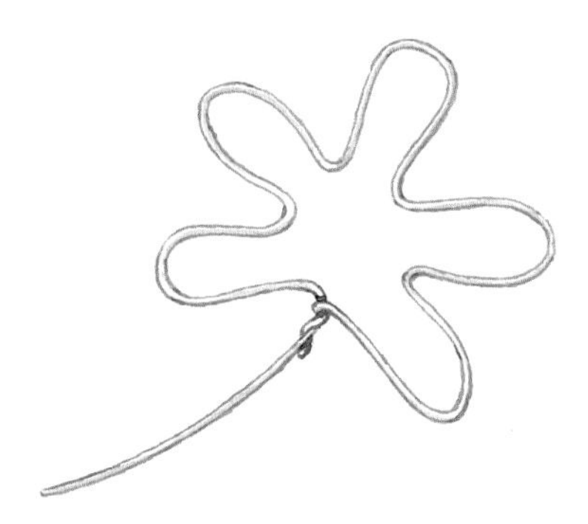

1 Cut a length of thin wire and bend into the shape you want.

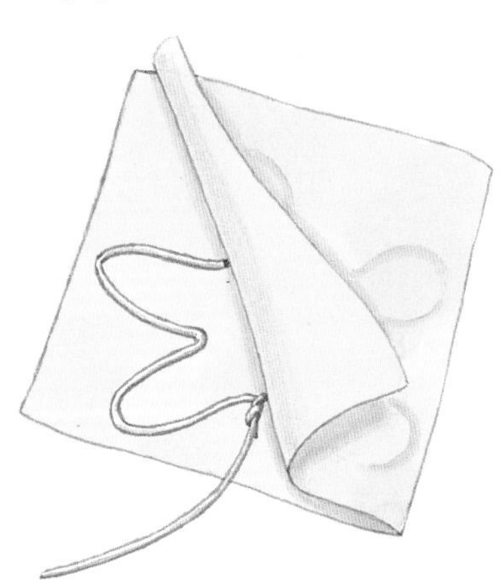

2 Cut a piece of tissue paper large enough to fold over the wire shape and cover both sides. Using a glue stick, cover the tissue in glue, taking care not to tear it. Put the wire shape inside and press down. Cut around the edge of the wire.

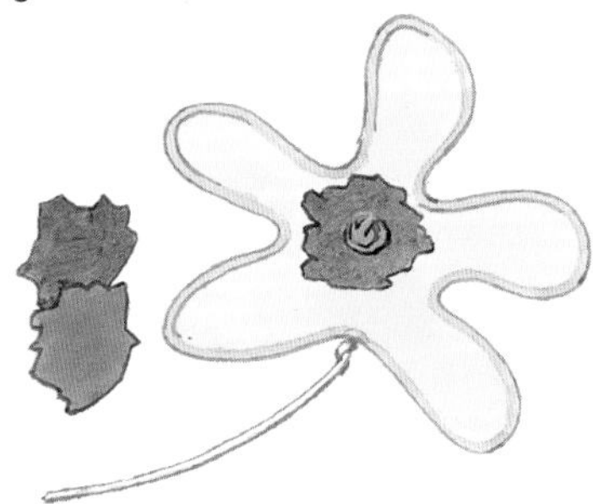

3 Glue on tissue paper in contrasting colors to add further details.

Left and below: A little more time is required to make wire and tissue decorations, but they are unusual and striking so the recipient is sure to be delighted and impressed. These decorations can be used on a tag, card, or seed pack or attached to a long piece of wire and pushed in among the leaves on a houseplant.

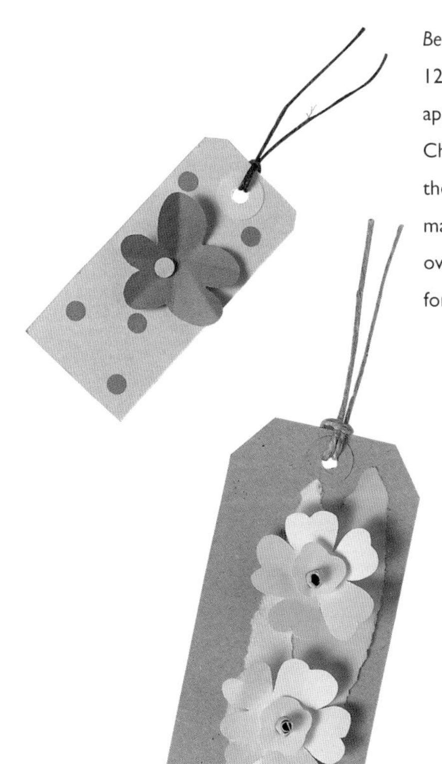

Below left and right: Using the motifs on page 120 and 121 as a template, you can cut out appropriate shapes such as flowerheads, leaves, or Christmas trees from colored paper. Either glue these to appropriately colored luggage labels or make them big enough to use as tags in their own right. A leaf shape makes a perfect gift tag for a green gift. For a natural look use nature's

Left, right, and below: One of the easiest and quickest ways to make an appropriately green tag is to glue something you have found in the yard or on a walk to the front of the tag: try a little fresh flower if the gift is to be given immediately. If not, use dried flower heads, little bunches of twigs, tiny stones, or a leaf. Only a little more effort is required to press and gild a leaf (see page 73) or to press flat flower heads, such as pansies, and attach them to a tag.

colors of green and brown and attach your tags with garden string or raffia. For a more colorful effect choose strongly colored scraps of paper to cut out flowers, leaves, hearts, and stars. For a different look, try sewing paper motifs to the tag instead of gluing them. Use contrasting colored thread and adjust the tension on your sewing machine so the stitches work on paper.

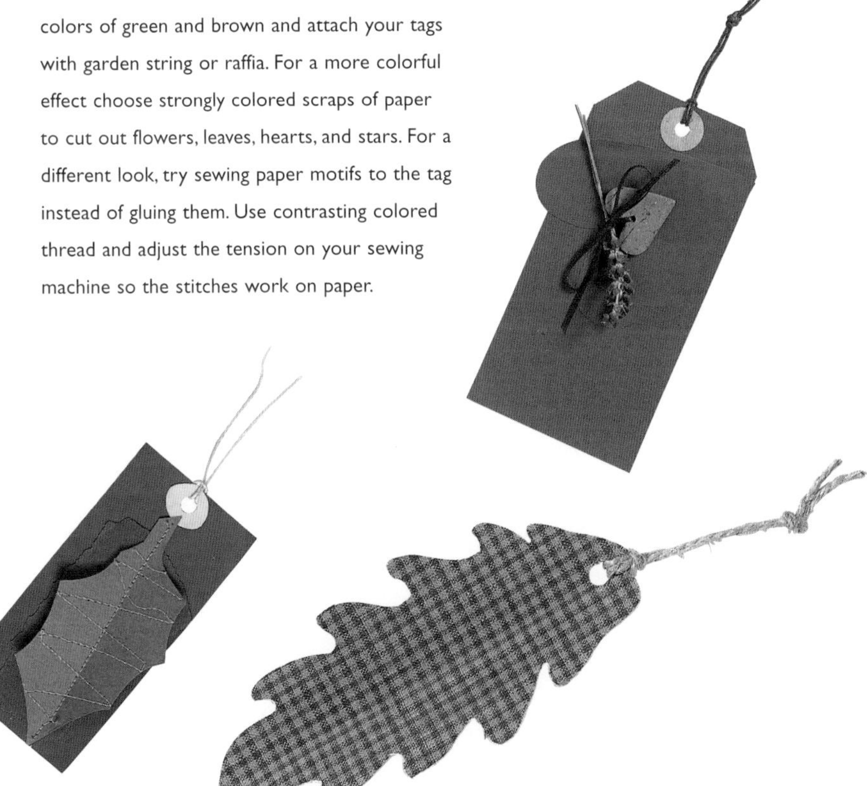

Below: A tag can swiftly be turned into a striking and attractive greetings card by gluing it to a piece of folded cardboard in a contrasting or complementary color. This card has quite an elaborate tag attached to it, but one gilded leaf can be equally effective. You can make a card like this and write the relevant care notes (see page 124) for your green gift inside.

Decorating pots

An unusual container can often be the inspiration for a really memorable green gift, plus the recipient gets an attractive pot or basket to keep. Look for interesting containers when visiting garden centers, florists, or antique shops. But don't limit your ideas to the conventional – you can find containers for plants in the most unlikely places. Everything from birdhouses (see page 68) to shopping baskets (see page 54) can be used. And don't forget wheelbarrows (page 46), watering cans (page 52), and buckets (page 53)!

Many containers can be painted to create a truly unique effect. Check out the local hardware store for small pots of paint suitable for outdoor use. You should find a good selection suitable for painting wooden and terracotta containers. You can either paint the whole pot or windowbox one color, or paint on patterns or pictures. Try painting blades of grass around the base of a pot with little flowers springing up between. Or for a more formal effect, stencil patterns or use masking tape to create a striped or checkered effect. If you don't mind the end result being heavy, you can cover a pot in concrete and press in shells, colored stones, or scraps of broken tile or pottery.

STRIPED AND CHECKERED POTS

1 Make sure the pot is clean and dry. Cut squares of masking tape and stick them to the pot in a checked pattern. For stripes, cut long strips of masking tape and place them around or down the pot.

2 Make sure the masking tape is smooth and firmly attached to the pot. Now paint the unmasked surfaces with the paint of your choice. A small, stiff brush is easiest to use.

3 Make sure the paint is completely dry before removing the masking tape. Peel it off carefully you do not damage the paint.

Left: Plain terracotta flowerpots are inexpensive to buy, come in all shapes and sizes and take paint very well. These have been painted all over first, left to dry then leaf patterns stencilled on top in a contrasting color.

Below left: Gold, silver or bronze paint looks great on terracotta. Use masking tape to create stripes or checked patterns.

Ideally, growing plants should be in pots with drainage holes at the bottom. Whenever possible, make drainage holes in the containers you buy and cover the holes with a good layer of stones or gravel so the holes don't get blocked with soil and the water can drain away. If pots outdoors can be raised on stones or the little "feet" you can buy at the garden center, so much the better. But if you can't make holes in your chosen container, then put at least 4 inches of drainage material in the bottom. And if your gift is liable to leak water, make sure you warn the recipient before they place it proudly on a polished surface!

MOSAIC POTS

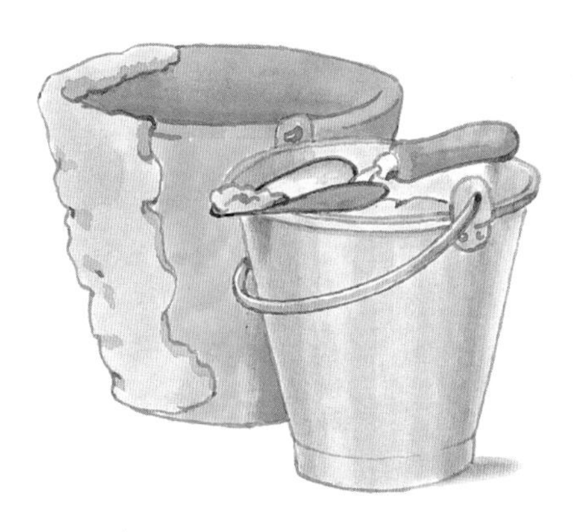

1 Buy a small bag of cement and mix it according to the manufacturer's instructions. Use a trowel to put the cement onto a clean garden pot. Aim for a layer about half an inch thick.

2 While the cement is still damp, begin decorating the pot by pushing in a selection of stones, shells, or broken china. Leave the pot to dry before planting.

STENCILED POTS

To get a good result, it is best to buy paper designed for cutting stencils from a craft store.

1 Choose a shape for your stencil. It is best to select a simple shape – a leaf is ideal. Transfer the shape on to stencilling paper and cut it out using a craft knife.

2 A straight-sided terracotta pot is ideal for stenciling. Make sure it is clean. Paint a base color all over the pot and let it dry. If the pot has a rim, paint that a contrasting color.

3 Put the stencil on the pot and secure it with masking tape. Stipple paint through the stencil using a dry brush. Move the stencil and repeat, aiming for a random effect. Make sure you do not smudge one pattern when working on the next.

Motifs

Use the motifs shown here for making stencils, tags, and greetings cards. The easiest way to duplicate the motifs is by photocopying them. If you have access to a photocopier which enlarges and reduces, you can also alter the size of the motif. If you can't get to a photocopier, use tracing paper to copy the motif.

Calendar

EARLY SPRING

- Sow in warmth half-hardy annuals (including climbers), herbs, and vegetables for use in containers
- Plant alpine garden containers to give in the fall
- Plant a cactus garden for a fall gift
- Buy primulas and other spring flowers for containers
- Buy flowering bulbs in pots

LATE SPRING

- Sow annuals in pots/trays for use in containers and outdoors for cutting
- Prick out (transplant) young seedlings
- Sow more herb seeds and vegetables for containers
- Buy perennial herbs in pots
- Plant herb containers
- Plant young vegetables (bought or self-grown) in containers
- Buy young herbaceous perennials for containers or cutting
- Sow sunflower seeds
- Plant hardy containers for summer
- Propagate hostas by division
- Plant and train topiary shapes

EARLY SUMMER

- Buy young bedding plants for summer containers
- Buy tender perennials for summer containers
- Pick herb leaves for drying or freezing and for wreaths
- Continue to train topiary
- Sow seeds of biennials to flower the following summer
- Buy flowering houseplants and outdoor climbers for pots

LATE SUMMER

- Pick leaves of herbs for drying
- Cut flower heads (lavender, hydrangeas, etc.) for drying
- Cut seedheads for saving seed
- Order and buy bulbs
- Plant strawberries in containers to give next year

EARLY FALL

- Plant prepared hyacinths and narcissi for Christmas flowering
- Plant containers with bulbs for forcing indoors
- Gather materials from yard and field for fall decorations
- Plant lily bulbs in deep containers
- Plant strawberries in containers
- Plant containers for winter interest
- Pick and store fruit for baskets

LATE FALL

- Plant tulip bulbs in containers for spring flowering
- Plant containers with bulbs for spring flowering outdoors
- Buy foliage houseplants for fall/winter gifts
- Plant lily bulbs in containers
- Plant winter interest containers
- Pick and store fruit for baskets
- Gather materials for winter decorations

EARLY WINTER

- Plant tulip bulbs in containers for late spring flowering
- Buy scented houseplants for winter gifts
- Buy pot-grown Christmas trees to decorate
- Gather materials from garden and countryside for wreath-making and decorations

LATE WINTER

- Plant containers with bulbs in flower or bud
- Buy scented houseplants
- Buy seeds to sow or give in spring
- Cut branches and twigs for flowering indoors

Care notes

Many of the green gifts described in this book will live for a long time given the right care. To help your friends and family get the most from your gift, give a copy of the relevant care notes with your present. Either photocopy the notes you want or copy them out in your own handwriting. Make a tag to put them on. You will also find these notes useful to make sure your gift looks its best when the time comes to present it.

PRIMROSES AND PRIMULAS

- Stand containers with holes in base in a shallow dish indoors. Raise off the ground if kept outside.
- Stand plants in a cool and light position indoors. Shelter from rain and cold winds if placed outside.
- Keep out of direct sun and drafts.
- Keep soil moist but don't overwater as roots may rot.
- Feed liquid fertilizer once a fortnight.
- Remove dead flowers and leaves regularly.
- When flowering is over, plant in a shady place outdoors. Plants should flower again next spring.
- **CAUTION** some people are allergic to the indoor plant *Primula obconica*.

SEEDS

for outdoor sowing

- Sow in a prepared seed bed of well-raked, level soil with a little added fertilizer.
- Scatter seeds thinly in drills (shallow trenches) either in straight rows or in a pattern.
- Cover with soil and water thoroughly.
- Protect the seed bed from cats and birds.
- Thin the seedlings when they germinate.

SEEDS

for indoor sowing

- Sow in trays or pots using potting medium sold commercially especially for seeds.
- Mix fine seeds with sand and press them into the compost. Cover larger seeds with a layer of medium.
- Water well after sowing and keep medium moist.
- For fine seeds cover trays or pots with plastic to conserve moisture.
- Keep at an even temperature and out of direct sun.
- Transplant seedlings when big enough to handle.
- Protect from cold, especially frost, until hardened off.

SEEDLINGS

- Keep seedlings well watered but not sodden.
- Spray with water if they are wilting.
- Stand them out of direct sun and sheltered from cold (especially if not hardy).
- Feed a diluted liquid fertilizer every two weeks.
- Stand pots on gravel to avoid slugs and snails.
- Pot on into a bigger container, or outdoors, when the roots fill the pot.

TULIPS

- Keep indoor tulips in pots in a cool, light room. A windowsill without strong sun is ideal.
- Turn the pot to prevent uneven growth.
- Stand outdoor pots in a partly shaded position, sheltered from wind and rain.
- Water moderately indoors, keeping water off the buds, but do not soak soil.
- Do not water outdoor containers in very cold weather. Check the soil does not dry out as the weather warms up.
- Remove dead flowers regularly.
- After flowering, put indoor containers outside. When leaves have withered, plant the bulbs or store dry until the fall. Do not use indoors again.
- Lift bulbs from outdoor pots and treat in same way.

HERBS

- Grow herbs in a sheltered, sunny spot.
- Plant in a well-drained, fertile soil, either in the flowerbed or in containers.
- Keep well watered and fed in the summer, but quite dry in winter.
- Pinch out the tips of shoots regularly to keep new leaves being produced. Remove flower buds if you are growing for culinary use.

SUNFLOWER COMPETITION

- Sow three seeds spaced out and about half an inch deep in a 3-inch pot.
- Put the pot on a warm windowsill indoors and water to keep the soil moist.
- When the germinated seedlings each have a pair of "true" leaves, remove all but the strongest seedling.
- Move this seedling into a large pot when its roots almost fill the little pot. Use soil-based potting medium, firm it in and water well.
- In early summer, put the pot outside in a sunny sheltered place, keep it well watered and feed with a liquid fertilizer once a week.
- Pinch out the side shoots to encourage strong growth from the main stem.
- Use soft twine to tie the plant to a support if needed.
- Choose a date to measure each of the plants.

CLIMBING FRAMES

- Stand pots outside in a sheltered but sunny spot for the summer.
- Keep well watered and liquid feed once a week while flowering.
- Remove dead and faded flowers.
- Twist growing shoots around supports and tie in.
- Discard annuals after flowering.
- Rest perennials by watering much less and ceasing to feed at the end of summer.
- Bring tender perennials such as plumbago and passion flower inside for the winter.
- In spring, prune plants which have overwintered and begin feeding them again.

HOSTAS

- Stand containers in a shady place outside.
- Keep well watered and liquid feed every two weeks when in growth.
- Protect against slugs and snails by greasing the rim of the pot and putting sand around the plants.
- Remove faded flower stems to encourage leafy growth.
- Leave pots outside all year but make sure soil will not freeze through if it is frosty.
- Early in the year, scrape away some soil and put a layer of fresh soil and general fertilizer on top.
- Divide plants in spring if you wish to have more hostas. Grow on the divided plants in smaller pots.

LILIES

- Place the pot in sun or semi-shade sheltered from strong winds if outside or in a cool room indoors.
- Always keep the soil moist. Never let it dry out.
- Feed with a liquid fertilizer occasionally.
- Provide supports for tall growing types.
- Watch for aphids and spray if necessary.
- Remove faded flowers and cut the stems down at the end of the flowering season.
- Store bulbs in dry peat or similar and plant out in the garden in the fall or repot for next summer.

VEGETABLES

- Stand the planted container in a sheltered and sunny place, but not somewhere so hot that it will dry out quickly. Move it out of all-day sun in summertime.
- Water at least once a day and never let the soil dry out.
- If a late frost threatens, protect plants with horticultural fleece or plastic.
- Liquid feed regularly once or twice a week using a diluted fertilizer.
- Support plants as they grow if necessary and remove dead leaves.
- Watch for aphids and other pests or diseases. Use an organic spray if treatment is required.
- Gather crops as soon as they become edible: go for quality, not size!

SUMMER HOUSEPLANTS

- Stand the plants in a light, draft-free position but not in direct sun.
- Water frequently. Take care to keep water off the leaves of African violets.
- Feed every two weeks during summer to encourage continuous flowering.
- Remove dead flower sprays regularly.
- Cut off any diseased leaves cleanly.
- Spray any aphids with a houseplant insecticide.
- When flowering is over and days shorten, water much less frequently.
- Plants may survive the winter if kept fairly dry and frost-free.

POTS OF COLOR

- Put containers in a sunny spot.
- Keep the soil well watered and liquid feed once a week.
- Remove dead flowers and leaves.
- Watch for pests and diseases and treat.
- Take cuttings of tender perennials such as fuchsias and geraniums in late summer if you want to overwinter plants for the following year.

STRAWBERRY POTS

- Stand the container in a sunny position.
- Protect the flowers from frost if necessary.
- Water regularly and copiously and liquid feed weekly while the plants are flowering and fruiting.
- Protect ripening fruit from birds.
- Pick fruit as it ripens to encourage more to form.
- Replace plants each year for best results. Propagate by planting runners in small pots while they are still attached to the parent plant. Detach them when they are well rooted (4-6 weeks).

TOPIARY

- Stand the container either indoors or out in summer. If the plant is hardy, it can stay outside over winter.
- Snip untidy shoots with a pair of scissors to keep the shape smooth.
- Twine new long shoots into the framework and tie in if necessary.
- Feed and water regularly to ensure strong growth of the foliage.
- If the topiary is indoors, turn it toward the light at intervals to keep growth even.
- Don't feed in winter, and reduce watering.
- Remove dead leaves.

ALPINES

- Stand containers, preferably at about waist height, in a sunny place. Alpines can tolerate wind exposure.
- Water the plants well in hot, dry weather.
- Remove any weeds that appear.
- Trim plants back if they become invasive.
- Protect plants from wet in winter, but let plenty of air circulate around them. A sheet of glass propped above the plants will help.

CACTI

- Stand cacti in strong light indoors: sun during winter months will not hurt them.
- Move the bowl outside in summer if possible. Choose a sheltered, sunny spot.
- From mid-spring to late summer water thoroughly when the soil dries out.
- Give an occasional liquid feed in summer.
- Gradually reduce watering in the fall and only water about once a month in winter.
- Keep plants cool but frost-free in winter – except for hairy cacti, which need to be kept at a minimum temperature of 60°F.

FALL BOXES AND POTS

- Position in a site sheltered from cold winds.
- Keep containers clear of overhanging roofs or trees so water does not drip on them.
- Water containers only when dry.
- If frost or snow is threatened, cover plants with a tent of horticultural fleece or similar light material. Remove protection when temperature rises.
- Protect roots from freezing by wrapping container closely with bubble plastic or sacking.

HYDRANGEAS

- In summer keep the plant cool and moist.
- Use rainwater for watering if you have hard tap water.
- Feed every two weeks with a liquid feed from spring to fall.
- Mist the leaves in dry conditions.
- Prune in spring by removing old or thin shoots and cut back flowered stems by half.
- Keep fairly dry in winter if indoors.
- Repot if necessary in spring, especially indoor ones.
- Support flower stems if they become too heavy.
- Protect new shoots on outdoor plants from frost.

INDOOR GARDEN

- Water very sparingly – keep the roots just moist.
- Use liquid feed at half strength about once a month (more often if the plants are in flower).
- Stand the pots in plenty of light in a cool place.
- Beware of cold drafts and don't leave pots behind curtains at night.
- Mist leaves several times a week or stand pots on trays of wet gravel.
- Wipe over large, non-hairy leaves to remove dust.

BULBS TO GROW INDOORS

for bulbs prepared for forcing

- Choose a container deep enough to allow root growth. It need not have drainage holes at the base.
- Put a layer of moist bulb fiber or peat-based potting medium about 2 inches deep in the bottom.
- Place the bulbs on top of the soil, close together but not touching, and continue to fill until the tips of the bulbs just show above the soil.
- Cover the bowl with black plastic to keep it dark and put in a cool, frost-free place.
- Move the bowl into a light, but shaded, position when the shoots are about 1 inch high. This is usually after 8-14 weeks). Increase warmth and light gradually. Do not put the bulbs in a very warm room.
- Turn the bowl regularly to keep the growth straight.
- Water just enough to keep the soil moist.
- Support flower heads with thin sticks or decorative twigs if they are top-heavy. Cut off dead flower heads.
- Let the leaves die back gradually after flowering; some liquid feed in the water at this stage will produce better bulbs for next year.
- When the foliage has withered, the bulbs can be planted outside – do not try to force them again.

BULBS TO GROW OUTDOORS

- Plant bulbs either directly in beds or grassland in the yard, or in outdoor containers.
- Make sure containers have drainage holes in the bottom and some drainage material in the base.
- Use ordinary potting soil in containers and protect them from frost in bad weather.
- Plant the bulbs deeply so their tops are well covered – a general rule is twice their own height for large bulbs and once their own height for small ones.
- Pack bulbs closely in containers and plant in two layers for a spectacular show.
- Feed bulbs after flowering but remove bulbs from containers and plant outside for next year.

HYACINTHS

- Stand the pots in a cool, light place out of direct sun.
- Water the soil to keep it moist but not wet.
- Support heavy flowerheads.
- Remove flowering stems once they have faded.
- Plant the bulbs outdoors; do not try to grow them for indoor use again.

CHRISTMAS TREE

- Keep as cool as possible, away from sources of heat such as radiators or fires.
- Keep the soil moist and water regularly.
- Mist the foliage with water occasionally (unless this will damage the decorations).
- Put the tree outside as soon as possible and either leave it in the container, or plant it outdoors in the spring.

BULBS IN FLOWER

- Keep bulbs in a cool place so flowers will last longer.
- Stand the container in a shallow dish if it has drainage holes.
- Make sure the soil is moist but not too wet and keep water off leaves and flowers.
- Turn containers regularly to keep growth even.
- Support foliage and flowers if necessary.
- Let foliage die down naturally and give some liquid feed at this stage.
- Keep dried-off bulbs to plant out in the fall. Do not grow them again in containers.

JASMINE

- Stand pot in a cool, light place away from drafts.
- Water regularly and do not let the soil dry out.
- Feed every two weeks while in flower and in the fall.
- Stand the plant outside during the summer and keep well watered.
- Prune long stems after flowering to maintain shape.

STEPHANOTIS

- Keep in a light, warm room but not in direct sun.
- Stand the pot on a tray of wet gravel to increase the air humidity.
- Water moderately but do not soak.
- Feed every two weeks while growing.
- Pinch out shoot tips to keep the plant in shape and remove dead flowers.

GARDENIA

- Make sure the soil is moist at all times and mist the leaves. Stand the pot on a bed of wet pebbles to increase humidity when flowering.
- Place in bright light, especially in winter.
- Feed about every 2-3 weeks with a liquid fertilizer from late spring to fall.
- Repot if necessary in spring.

INDEX

AUTHOR'S ACKNOWLEDGMENTS

Very special thanks to Debbie Patterson for her enthusiasm and wonderful photographs that capture such a glorious quality of light and color; my neighbors and friends Penny and Robin Wade, Pat and Kenneth Pearson, Viv and Tom Jestico for generously letting us use their beautiful gardens and props; Peter, Paul, and their team at the Conservatory in Richmond, Surrey, for their help; Alan King and Vincent Charlton at 30-32 Hill Rise, Richmond for kindly lending the gnome, page 47, and yellow bucket, page 53, from their interesting selection of antiques. Thank you also to Paperchase, V V Rouleaux, The Dining Room, Clifton Nurseries, and finally to Prue Bucknall for the excellent, clear design, and Janet Slingsby for making this book possible, for her valuable input, and much appreciated hard work.